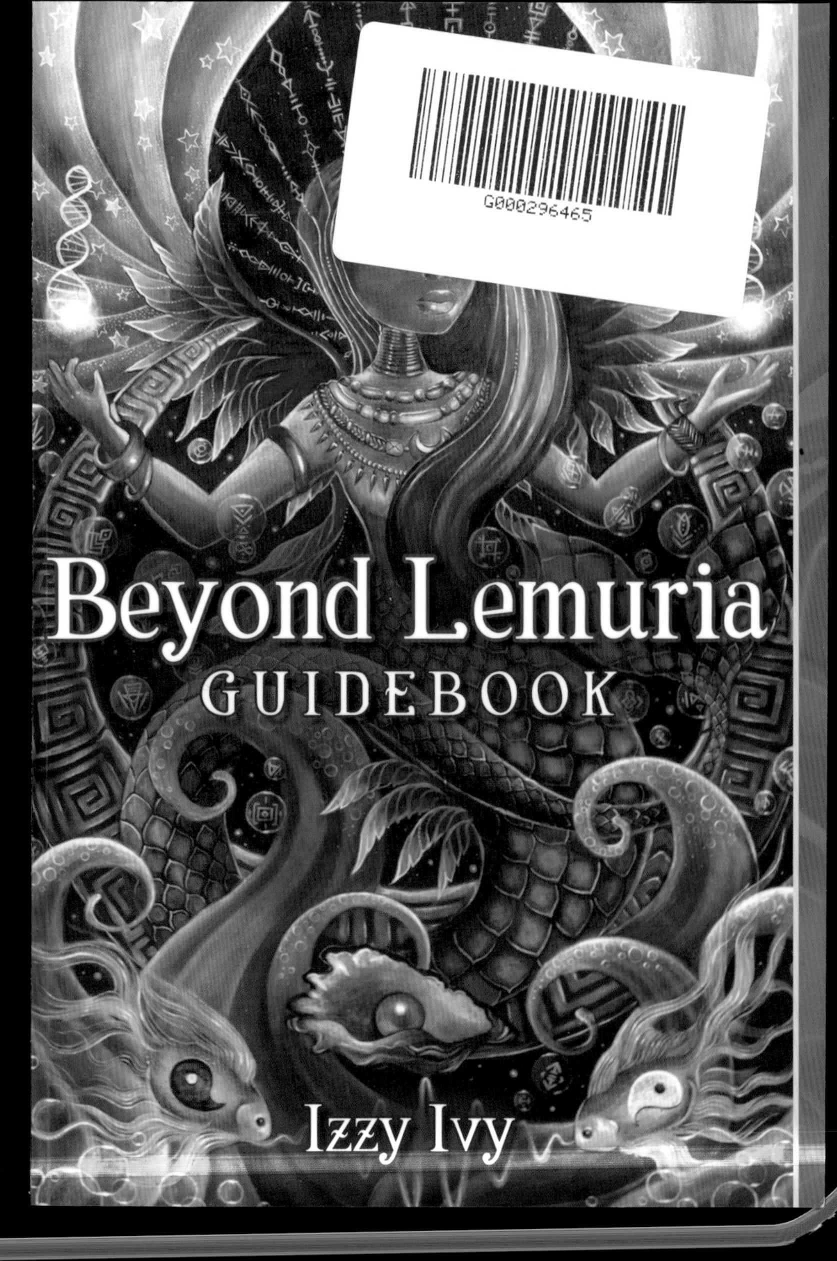
G000296465
Beyond Lemuria
GUIDEBOOK
Izzy Ivy

Beyond Lemuria

ORACLE CARDS

Text and images by

Izzy Ivy

BEYOND LEMURIA

This printing 2021

Published by Blue Angel Publishing®
80 Glen Tower Drive, Glen Waverley,
Victoria, Australia 3150
E-mail: info@blueangelonline.com
Website: www.blueangelonline.com

Text and images by Izzy Ivy

Edited by Leela J. Williams

ISBN: 978-1-925538-83-0

Contents

Preface..7
Introduction..13

CARD MEANINGS

CHAKRA CARDS

1. Earth Star Chakra: Initiation 32
2. Root Chakra: Ground and Centre 33
3. Sacral Chakra: Core of Creation 34
4. Solar Plexus Chakra: Radiant Illumination.......35
5. Heart Chakra: Unfurling Back to Love.............36
6. High Heart Chakra: Ecstatic Bliss 37
7. Throat Chakra: Express Your Truth................38
8. Third Eye Chakra: Pineal Perspective.............39
9. Crown Chakra: The Unlimited Self..................40
10. Soul Star Chakra: Merging with the Divine...41

ELEMENTAL CARDS

11. Aether: The Seamless Unspeakable 44
12. Water: The Overflow.......................................45
13. Air: Paradigm Shift...46
14. Earth: Nurture Nature......................................47
15. Fire: Solerus Sublime..48
16. Loving Compassion...49
17. Awakened Awareness.......................................51

SEED CARDS

18. Alignment....................56
19. Balanced Forces....................58
20. Beyond the Mind....................60
21. Communication Co-creation....................62
22. Crystal Keys....................64
23. Endless Opportunities....................66
24. Evolution....................68
25. Freedom....................70
26. Full Spectrum....................72
27. Furred & Feathered Friends....................75
28. Gracious Receptivity....................77
29. Harmonic Flight....................80
30. Healing....................83
31. Home....................86
32. Internal Explorer....................88
33. Journey to Wholeness....................90
34. Life-Force Energy....................92
35. Lumin Essence....................94
36. Manifestia....................97
37. Mount Shasta....................99
38. New Blueprints....................101
39. Our Ancient Future....................103
40. Radical Expansion....................105
41. Realm Bridger....................107
42. Reclaim Your Energy....................109
43. She of the Lotus....................112
44. Shine Your Light....................115
45. Star Seed Elemental....................117
46. Star Seer....................119
47. Stepping Through....................121

48. Surrender..123
49. The Infinite..125
50. The Portal Keeper..127
51. The Sound of the Universe...........................131
52. The Violet Flame..133
53. Transformation...135
54. Trust Your Innocence.......................................136
55. Unique Gifts..138
56. Vulnerability..140

About Izzy Ivy..143
Also available from Blue Angel Publishing.........144

Preface

NOTIONS OF THE MICROCOSM and macrocosm and how they are inextricably linked are often present in my paintings and the words of Lemurian wisdom that come through me. But what is it about this fractal geometry that is so important?

This oracle explores and offers keys for the shifting paradigm we are undeniably experiencing on Earth right now. It is not the first time the Lemurians have experienced a dramatic ending due to extreme duality and the overzealous misuse of power. They assure us that we can gracefully do it differently this time around and that change starts within us. They offer us tools for navigating and transmuting the shadows and systems behind what urges a person, and a collective society, to behave so disharmoniously.

Lemuria was the original paradise. If we are to allow Eden to flourish on Earth once again, we need to return to living harmoniously with nature, just as our ancestors did for thousands of years. We are already aware that we need to live more sustainability, but do we know what that means? Humanity is leaning on finite resources. Not only will those resources run out, but the process of constantly taking them from the earth is creating undeniable problems for our planet.

For any living being to exist, it needs to generate an equal balance of 'give' for its 'take'. This is like the in and out of breathing. We breathe in oxygen and breathe out carbon dioxide, while plants symbiotically do the opposite of this. The toroidal field of energy around the body represents this with energy coming in and going out, receptive and assertive.

Earth has maintained equilibrium for billions of years. It is true, there are naturally fluctuating ebbs and flows, but in the last two hundred years, we have seen dramatic changes that are a major spike on the graph of Gaia's history. If we continue like this and don't make the shift now, it will be almost impossible to turn back.

Bringing this back to the macro and the micro, the big and the small, with a focus on *self-generating power,* the key to tipping back the balance is the use of infinite sources, rather than finite ones. Realigning Earth and restoring harmony is a big task, and there is much talk about working together to bring about this change. Working together is a major key in creating transformation, and many communities are seeding the realities they wish to see. As more and more people do this, there is a wider ripple-effect, and we all start to awaken each other. However, before we get to that point, there is another level to address: the individual.

You may be aware of the direct link between the macro and the micro, that what we express in our inner world we create in our outer world. But what if we take it a step further and consider what happens when we self-generate our power in a way that taps into infinite sources?

Much of my mission of inspiration and the core message of this oracle is about finding what fills you up and overflows your cup and what happens when you follow your bliss and makes you shine. We all have things we can do that do not tire us, where even after hours of focus, we still feel fully charged and inspired. Even if you are still figuring out your life purpose, you can introduce more 'flow' into your life. We can balance productivity with fluid tranquillity, where hours vanish, and the act of doing energises rather than exhausts you.

Ecstatic dance is a fantastic example of this. Here, you are expending energy as you move your body. But, the act of letting your soul dance you, and freely allowing the rhythm to move your very essence gives you a huge amount of energy. Personally, I find I can dance and express physical energy in a way I would never be able to do in a gym. It is no surprise that our ancestors danced on the land in a way that is not so dissimilar. I recently received an intuitive message that dancing on the land would help the grace of the shift back to balance on earth. I describe ecstatic dance as 'letting spirit dance you' and now see what it symbolises. It is self-generating power.

The project you are inspired by, the painting you are compelled in your heart to express, the aliveness you feel despite possible challenges … aligning with your passion gifts you with unbounding energy to create and generate exponentially. That doesn't happen when we are doing something we aren't really into.

So, find what fills you up. What is your infinite overflow? Look for the skill, quality or interest where what you give almost never tires you. Indeed, we are still in human form, so we do get tired eventually, but doing what we love is the closest thing to infinite giving. I experienced the notion of this, and the Lemurians did have access to the infinite (and they lived for thousands of years).

As we shift our awareness to the macrocosm, the bigger picture collective, we can conclude that if we, as individuals, are naturally creating our own energy, power, light or joy by honing our awareness, we are going to be less reliant on external needs or taking more than is a healthy balance.

Relationships based on overflow result in balanced connections and expansion. When we feel energetically depleted, and try to 'fill our gaps' it can lead to co-dependent relationships and unhealthy food choices. As we raise our vibration, our expanded consciousness inspires us to question where our food comes from and the energetic element of getting it to our plates. In general, consumerism taps into our need (conscious or otherwise) for something outside ourselves. Western culture is based on this, and that is a major reason why it is normal for an individual to reach for something that will give them energy, power, or a sense of nurture – even if it is just for a fleeting moment. Consuming on such a large scale is a direct cause of the problem we are facing on Earth.

What if we could self-generate our power, as the Lemurians are inspiring us to consider?

When we are aware of our life purpose or had a glimpse of where we have abundant energy, there is overflow instead of obligation. When we work collectively, as united overflowing individuals, people can really create magic. It is as if each person is a different puzzle piece of the 'work' they feel they are here to do, and all practical elements of existence can be taken care of in a way that is enjoyable and in alignment with that which we happily fill our lives.

As the paradigm shifts, skills that help keep one's vibration high will be important. Healers, artists, musicians and designers will be integral to community, as necessary as practical tradespeople. As we continue to raise our vibration, some of the very third-dimensional roles will become unnecessary.

It's almost as if half this oracle deck is about cultivating what makes you shine, and the other half is about moving the blocks. Half of the work is learning to self-generate power/energy, and the rest is about freeing your shadows in a playful, optimistic way, helping you navigate the things that take you out of your centre and get in the way of your natural birthright to self-generate.

Shadows create triggers that are based on past traumas and drain our self-generating energy. When we live with awareness around cultivating our energy (information on this throughout the guidebook), we realise the importance of doing healthy shadow work, so we have clear channels to abundant life-force energy. It also creates harmonious communication and connection with others, which is key to working together as we ground the reality we collectively want to see.

There are many facets to aligning ourselves with life-force energy, also known as Reiki energy. When we maintain awareness of our energy, we cultivate sovereignty. Whereas, the journey of bringing any fractured parts of oneself back to the centre is about restoring wholeness. These fractures may occur due to trauma and returning to wholeness is a more integrated way of saying healing. Other terms may be used, but they all aim to claim one's birthright to connect to infinite sources within ourselves and to all that lights up our heart and spirit.

RADIATING LIGHT

This oracle has unfolded piece by piece as I wandered down the path of following the whispers of my soul. As I embraced the role of a realm bridging messenger, the universe continued to gift me information to share through the medium that is my overflow.

As I come to completion with the creation of deck, I have been shown multiple visions and synchronistic confirmations in the physical world about the importance of the Great Central Sun. It aligns perfectly with the theme of the macro-microcosm we are sharing here. I was shown the importance of the sun in the centre of our galaxy, the sun in our solar system, the one inside each of us (our solar plexus or dantien) and that there is also one in the centre of our Mother Earth (note, these are all of an overlaying higher dimensional plane).

I saw how they are all inextricably linked and how we could access infinite energy from connecting to this pure bright light. Working with Reiki and other energetic modalities for over a decade, I have gleaned an awareness of where this *highest brightest light* originated. I glimpsed a deeper understanding of the 'golden ones' and their emergence from the centre of Gaia as the vibration on Earth reached a certain frequency. I also saw how the Lemurians were connected to the golden ones, and are perhaps one and the same, as they are known to reside beneath the surface of the earth in sacred places around the planet, the main one being Mount Shasta.

As the pieces came together, I realised why every painting I have ever created contains stars — because when we remember, we all have the capacity to be a star (a sun) and can self-generate our light and power when we connect to the infinite.

By allowing our soul to radiate through us, in whichever medium we choose or whatever name we wish to give it, and attuning to the highest frequency of light, we can create universes of the realities we wish to see. We create rippling patterns, that influence the macrocosm, as the infinite dances us, radiating fractal geometry into the bigger picture perspective.

Introduction

Welcome to the realm of Lemuria, a magical place infused with an abundance of life-force energy, fertile lands, lush rainforests, crystalline waterfalls and beings who so gracefully dance with the tides of nature and the ebb and flow of life. There is no scarcity as all that is required can be created at will. In essence, Lemuria is an elevated state of being ... a dreaming that sees beyond the dream.

> *Lemuria is the knowing of the universe and all her stars, the all that came before and ever will be, the iridescent shimmer of remembering what we came here to do, the awakening beyond the veil of the mundane, the journey back to wholeness in honour of every part of who we are. This is the unfurling, back to our hearts, the sovereign incarnation, the interconnectedness of existence. This is home.*

WHAT IS LEMURIA?

Many of us are familiar with Atlantis, a lost civilisation that disappeared into the Atlantic Ocean many thousands of years ago. Atlantis was home to a highly evolved race of beings whose technology was centred around the power of crystals. They harnessed natural energy in a way is currently unfathomable to us.

Also known as Mu, Lemuria was another civilisation that existed on the planet at the same time or just before Atlantis. Located in the Pacific Ocean, its residents were of a gentler, more earth-based nature. They also worked with the crystalline forces of minerals and the planets. They sought to be in harmony with life rather than the hierarchical power that would push evolution to the threshold and eventually bring extinction across the planet.

Lemuria and Atlantis may have resided in physical reality. There are also accounts that imply these civilisations exist or existed in a multidimensional overlay to the reality with which we are more familiar. Whatever you believe, their lessons, stories and understanding of the universe and the future of humanity is accessible to us. When we work with the energies of their blueprints, as mythical stories, archetypes or as a reality that is even more true than the physical, as our indigenous kin may inspire us to see, we can find our way to their wisdom.

You may be familiar with Lemurian Quartz crystals, or *seed crystals* as they are also known as they are found buried in the ground. These crystals are indented with lines — ridges and furrows — and it is said they hold Lemurian wisdom that will one day be significant to a future civilisation.

There seems to be an influx of Lemurian incarnates on Earth right now. Another view is that the archetypal message these beings carry is showing up in increasing prevalence. There is a remembering and a realisation that the keys for a sustainable future are in the ancient roots of our ancestors and the lost civilisations that came before. The Lemurian archetype has been portrayed in Hollywood films such as *Avatar* and more recently, *Valerian*. This shows how the Lemurian imagery and information is droppleting throughout our culture at this time.

Right now, we are facing a parallel story of Lemuria and Atlantis. By working against the laws of nature rather than with them, humanity heads toward the possibility of erasing life on Earth. The message of the Lemurians is that we can do it differently this time. The shift starts from within ourselves. As we move through our own trauma, triggers and power struggles, we create space for light and life force. We can build on our true inner-sent power and embrace the possibility of bridging heaven and earth.

From this vibration, we have a starting point. By holding the vision, not only can we bring Mama Earth and her civilisations back into balance, but we will create the Eden-like paradise this incredible blue planet can be.

MY JOURNEY WITH LEMURIA

There seems to be many ideas about what Lemuria was. I have always had a deep connection with this magical place and have received downloads, visions and memories of an incarnation in Lemuria. Thus, I feel I have witnessed their way or life, their environments and how they relate to the world.

When I started to expand my understanding of Lemurians, there was not a lot of information written about them. I delighted in the resonance I felt when I met others who shared similar encounters, as there was usually a significant thread of confirmation.

Embracing my life purpose as a healer and painter was directly connected to the realms of Lemuria. The images that unfurl on my canvas have been a beacon for folk who are likewise imbued with this remembering. As my connections expanded, I felt encouraged to ground my awareness further and was called to travel to significant vortices around the world where I could further explore the whisperings from this ancient future.

The messages of Lemuria and its residents have been the core of my life's work. Piece by piece, image by image, with personal learnings, growth and transmutation, a foundational way of living has unfolded. I feel honoured to have created a container for this wisdom and now share this universe with you in the form of an oracle deck.

WHO WERE THE LEMURIANS?

Lemurians were highly evolved beings with great telepathic ability. They had access to limitless life-force energy and could manifest and heal almost anything. They were multidimensional beings and could move between worlds or overlaying dimensions at will, including backwards and forwards in time. To them, all time was happening simultaneously, and they had direct access to the Akash, a living library where everything that ever was and ever would be could be accessed.

Lemurians were familiar with portals and traversed dimensions to gain information and share wisdom. They were deeply connected with other planets, aware of the balance and interconnectedness of all the activity that happens in the *macro-micro universe*. Often inhabiting the abyss in the spaces between perceivable matter, their particles and physical densities could transform as they chose. The way they could move through time and space means they also have access to this very moment, and their wisdom is gifted to us as we raise our vibrations to meet theirs.

As they could create anything at will, scarcity was not a factor in their reality. The natural land they lived in flourished and they didn't need to grasp or hold onto anything. Having immediate access to whatever they desired meant the need to own anything did not develop. They lived close to the incredible land and spent much of their time recharging their energetic resources by immersing themselves in the blissful emanations of nature.

They appeared tribal and were scantily clad as their body

temperature was perfectly attuned to that of their environment and there was no shame in nudity. Talismans adorned their body, as beautiful art was a way of containing significant information. They were shapeshifters and could disappear and reappear as they chose or as they moved through different dimensions. They held a deep connection and familiarity with crystals and worked with vibration to bridge spiritual and physical realms.

The Lemurians' main form was humanoid. They were tall with long limbs and transparent skin that had an iridescent shimmer. Depending on their evolution, they were strong, agile and often androgynous-looking. Some had 'hair' that looked like dreadlocks but was made of the same iridescent-white, semitransparent matter as their bodies. They were gentle beings who lived in their hearts and intuition was their guidance system for every moment of their life. You could see the depth of the universe in their large eyes, and they could raise the vibration of whatever environment they were in.

They didn't need to eat as they could bring energy directly into their bodies. The arts, dance, music, ceremony and metaphorical expression were keys to their everyday life. Community was vital and sharing the upbringing of children and having loving connections with several partners was not unusual.

They had close connections with mythical beings as the dimensions these beings resided in were similar. They were both of the earth and the etheric realm. They could fly, but they didn't need wings so unless it was for adornment, they preferred minimal appendages for a greater sense of lightness and freedom.

They had a deep connection with animals, plants, the weather and the elements. They are beings we can invite in, to balance Earth and our solar system. They were deeply connected to their ancestors, which were of star origin and shared traits and information with various star beings.

HOW DID IT END?

There are different accounts of what caused the demise of Lemuria and Atlantis, but I have learned that my visions of the land tearing up with cataclysmic earthquakes and tidal waves are not uncommon. Some say it was an energetic form of nuclear warfare, others that Atlantis was pushing their experiments of harnessing power to extremes. Their strong intent for accelerated evolution may have propelled both races into the higher dimensions. There are many opinions depending (perhaps) on whose perspective it is taken from.

I had a vision of Earth with two moons where the Atlanteans tried to harness energy from one, similar to how they worked with huge crystals and pyramids. But it was too powerful and shifted the magnetic core of the earth, the poles and the gravitational field.

On receiving the ominous intuition of this event, some of the beings of these lands were able to journey to other places across the globe. Many accounts suggest that the Lemurians travelled to the Americas, Pacific Islands, Australia and New Zealand, seeding the tribal, earth-centred peoples, while the Atlanteans travelled to Egypt, Greece, Central America and India seeding their monolithic cultures.

Although this happened many thousands of years ago, in another epoch, Lemuria is still alive in some of the high-vibrational vortices on the planet. Hawaii is said to be one of the last remaining parts of Lemuria. This is not hard to imagine due to the incredible degree of life-force energy present in nature there. Mount Shasta, in California, is also deeply connected to Lemuria. Many of the remaining Lemurians are said to live under this huge mountain in a fifth-dimensional paradise called Telos.

The teachings of the Lemurians are alive in the whisperings of ancient natural places. Those that live closely with the land, continue to dance and sing their mysteries, through plant medicines and when we are able to lift our vibration through meditation, dance and whatever brings us into the presence of our hearts.

When we can shift the beliefs and the stories that keep us small, we can move into our true purpose and freedom. When we follow our bliss and our heart of hearts and realise every little thing we do does make a difference, we can be the change — individually collectively and in the macro-micro scale beyond space and time.

HOW TO USE THESE CARDS

The shift back to bridging heaven and earth starts within us. We must tend to the garden inside ourselves before we can heal that which is outside of us. It is time to honour our own little piece of Eden. We can do this by becoming consciously aware of our actions, intentions and shadows.

Being able to swiftly bring our energy into balance when we are out of our heart-space and knowing how to wield our power and unique gifts are paramount in these times of potential transformation. Each card in this deck highlights a way we can anchor more light back onto planet Earth by working with the forces of duality (rather than against it) in lightness, sweetness, and with a childlike inquisitiveness.

I believe we all have the capacity to gain the knowledge we seek when we let go and drop into the collective archetypal ocean of all-knowing. I also believe we have the keys and the light codes within our aura to activate the most profound version of ourselves. While the card images have an accompanying message, their symbolism speaks to a different part of one's being. Much like deciphering a dream, these meanings may be different for each person. Thus, I invite you to look between the lines, consider how the cards make you feel and reflect on what the symbols and colours mean to you based on your personal connection and experiences.

ABOUT THE CARDS

You can use this deck the same way you would use any oracle, but there are some special features about these cards. The fifty-six cards are divided into three categories. There are ten chakra cards, seven elemental cards and thirty-nine seed cards. The cards are numbered for ease of reference.

CHAKRA CARDS

These cards represent the seven chakras we are familiar with plus the high heart, soul star and earth star. As we have evolved spiritually, three new energy-centres have revealed themselves. I often see these in my healing work, especially in those who are aligned with the call of their spirit.

Use these cards to work with the energy in one's energy field or aura. There are activation codes in the left-hand corner. When I was on the top of Mount Shasta, I was strongly guided to channel a painting, which is where (unexpectedly) these codes came through. There is one for each of the ten chakra cards. You can read more about this in the *Mount Shasta* card.

Along with the title and keywords, the guidebook includes an overall meaning and description for the chakra cards, as well as the following sections:

Restore: Suggestions for rebalancing, clearing or healing the chakra.

Themes: Areas to explore and filter the message of your reading through.

Healing Position: Place the card at this position on the body to activate the chakra.

Colour Wash: Visualise this colour washing over you as you work with the chakra.

ELEMENTAL CARDS

The first of these cards represent the five elements: *Air*, *Fire*, *Water*, *Earth* and *Aether*. I was also guided to include *Loving Compassion* and *Awakened Awareness*. Although not normally expressed as elements that form existence, I can see how they are similarly significant and are vital to creating an optimum reality, especially in ceremony.

Along with the title and keywords, there is an overall meaning and themes for each card. Use the elemental cards for working with the energy in one's environment. In the left-hand corner of each card, there are activation codes that use archetypal symbols for the elements. The symbols for *Loving Compassion* and *Awakened Awareness* came through during a co-creative ceremony with a brother sharing a similar journey and message at a sacred site in Bali.

It wasn't until I was drawing the diagrams (as the final refinement to this guidebook) that I realised the symbols I was guided to create combine to form a Merkabah! *Mer* means light. *Ka* means spirit. *Ba* means body. A Merkabah is a divine-light vehicle purportedly used by ascended masters to connect with and reach those in tune with the higher realms. The Merkabah represents the spirit-body as it is surrounded by counter-rotating fields of light that transport the spirit-body from one dimension to another.

This synchronicity is the perfect analogy to how this entire oracle has presented and unfurled itself through me. Had I known I would both paint and write this deck in the time I had and with everything else going on in my life, I could not have fathomed it. It has really shown me that when we get out of our own way, trust in the passions that make our soul sing, listen to our inner guidance, choose to find the silver lining in our challenges and allow ourselves to revel in our creativity — even just for a moment — it is amazing what can be birthed. That in itself is the perfect medicine of this offering.

SEED CARDS

Constituting the main body of the deck, the seed cards are varied, and their messages go into depth. These could be likened to Lemurian seed crystals, as each one is a container of information, like a Lemurian download that is ready to be unearthed. Along with the title and keywords, the guidebook includes an overall meaning and a divinatory meaning for each card.

CARD SPREADS AND READING LAYOUTS

LIFE TOOLKIT READINGS

Here is an array of quick and simple three-card spreads to help you with some extra insight as and when you need it. After choosing the most appropriate reading from the below list (or creating your own), enter a meditative space. Allow your breathing to deepen and slow while inviting a sense of being present in the now moment. As you shuffle the cards you can ask the questions associated with your chosen reading. Choose one card for each of the three questions Focus on the relevant question as you pick each card. Lay the cards face up in the order you pick them.

A message for today

Card 1: What should I be aware of?
Card 2: What can I grow from?
Card 3: Where should I put my energy?

The flow of life

Card 1: What am I here to bring into the world?
Card 2: What is the most relevant lesson I can grow from, right now?
Card 3: Where should I put my energy?

Life purpose

Card 1: What is at the core of what I love to do?
Card 2: What is in the way of me doing more of what I love?
Card 3: What should I be aware of for the most aligned opportunities?

Moving through triggered moments

Card 1: What is the core of the trigger?
Card 2: What can I do about it?
Card 3: What does the vision of wholeness look like?

Decision-making

Card 1: What does my mind choose?
Card 2: What does my heart sing?
Card 3: What does my body feel?

Manifestation

Card 1: What can I do to accelerate what I wish to manifest?
Card 2: What can I let go of to create space for this manifestation?
Card 3: What is the theme to be aware of for the most aligned opportunities?

Bringing in love

Card 1: How can I open my heart?
Card 2: What is blocking my heart?
Card 3: What current lesson will expand my heart?

Health

Card 1: What is bringing me out of wholeness?
Card 2: What can I do to bring in more life-force energy and encourage swifter healing?
Card 3: What vision can I hold to remind me of wholeness and health? (Here, consider the energy flow, character and colours of the card image)

Your most magical self

Card 1: What are the best tools for connecting to the Divine?

Card 2: Show me some insight into my spirit guides?

Card 3: What can I do to experience more magic in every moment?

Aura insights and clearing

Card 1: What is the most prominent theme for clearing my energy or body right now?

Card 2: What colours are my aura? Refer to the chakra cards to navigate the meaning of the predominant colours of the card you picked?

Card 3: What theme can best inspire me to keep my energy clear?

ENERGY-BODY INSIGHT CONSTELLATION

This reading uses the chakra system to navigate what is going on in the energy-body and presents insights that link into the root cause of an issue. By working with the chakra centres, another layer of more specific information can be generated. Relevant themes will be highlighted, based on what each chakra point is known to encompass.

For example, our throat centre relates to communication and self-expression. The card that presents itself in alignment with this area will be connected to this chakra's theme and area of the body. This deck includes ten chakra cards representing the seven chakras we are familiar with plus the high heart, soul star and earth star.

1. Separate the ten chakra cards from the deck.

2. Set the intention for the reading by asking for insight into your energetic system using the chakras as a guide.
3. Close your eyes and allow a number between one and ten to come into your mind's eye. Use the first number you think of when you do this. (We will use five as an example)
4. Shuffle the chakra cards and pick the number of cards that you intuited. (For our example we are picking five.) Place the cards face down in front of you.
5. Shuffle the rest of the deck and pick a card for each of the chakra cards. (Again, for our example, we are picking five.) Place the cards face down, next to the charka cards.
6. Without turning the cards over, intuitively match a card from the chakra card pile with a card from your second pile.
7. Turn the two cards over. Use the meanings in the guidebook to gain deeper insight into the core of an issue and how it is impacting your physical body and energy system.

CONSTELLATIONS

A constellation is a type of reading. A seed card can be combined with an elemental or chakra card to reveal more specific information. The constellations provide another layer to the message and give greater dimension to a reading. The two cards fit together to create extra facets of insight with greater detail.

AURA-HEALING CONSTELLATION

This is a healing rather than a reading, but it works well with the energy-body constellation above. As we go through life, we will inevitably experience trauma of different kinds. The effects of trauma can be held in our aura or energy field, and gradually move closer to the physical and come to affect the organs in that area. When we carry this baggage around with us, it can also affect us emotionally and trigger anxiety, depression or other symptoms. Therefore, it is important to clear your energy on a regular basis. There are many methods for doing this, reiki (which is said to have its roots in Lemurian healing) is one of them. This aura-healing constellation is another way to clear and balance the energy system for yourself and others.

The chakras can help us navigate the energy system around our bodies in its entirety. If they are working in good flow — spinning at the optimum pace and without blockages — then more life-force energy can move efficiently through the system. This has a direct link to our physical and emotional energy levels.

If you have just done an energy-body constellation, you can use the chakra cards from that reading. Alternatively, you can pick some of the chakra cards intuitively, with the intention of directing life-force energy to the areas where it is needed. Pick as many cards as feels relevant. You may do this by shuffling the cards, or if you know there is a chakra that needs some extra attention you can work with this.

1. Get yourself comfortable and lie down with the cards next to you.
2. Using the symbol on the left-hand side of the card, hover your palm over the card and draw this symbol over the whole card as if you are drawing with a beam of light. Repeat three times.
3. Place the card on the area of the body that is associated with this chakra. Do this with the intention of bringing that energy centre back into balance and wholeness in the light of the highest good.
4. See the colours of the card expand out through your whole aura as you place them on your body.

5. Do this for each card you have picked.
6. Lie back and enjoy the blissful feeling of receiving whatever you need to experience right now.

ELEMENTAL-PORTAL CONSTELLATION

This layout works with the energy of one's environment to rebalance, clear, protect and activate physical space. The seven elemental cards are perfect for holding space during ceremony. This formation can be used anywhere you would like to invite more life-force energy for healing and to lift the vibration, such as your home or your workspace. It is especially good for transforming areas of dissonance. When working with this spread, the themes of the chosen cards will encourage the appropriate energies to cultivate in the immediate environment.

1. Lay the seven elemental cards in a compass formation. Align *Earth, Air, Fire* and *Water* with the four directions (image side up) with Aether in the centre. Place *Loving Compassion* and *Awakened Awareness* on either side of the spread.

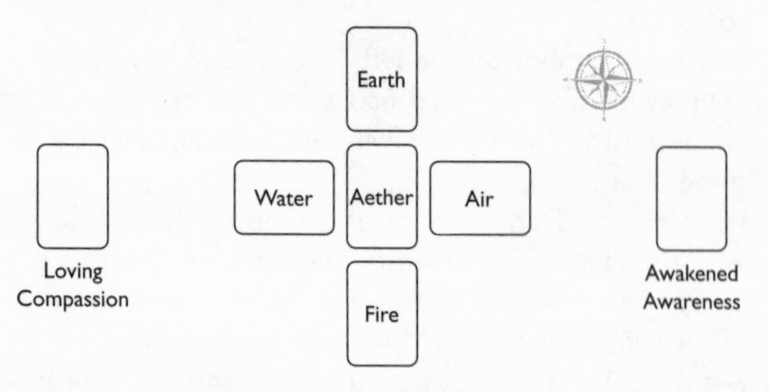

2. Set the intention for whatever you would like the environment to hold space for. E.g. energetic equilibrium.

3. Shuffle the rest of the deck and select five cards.
4. Without turning the five cards over, intuitively match each one with a card from the compass formation.

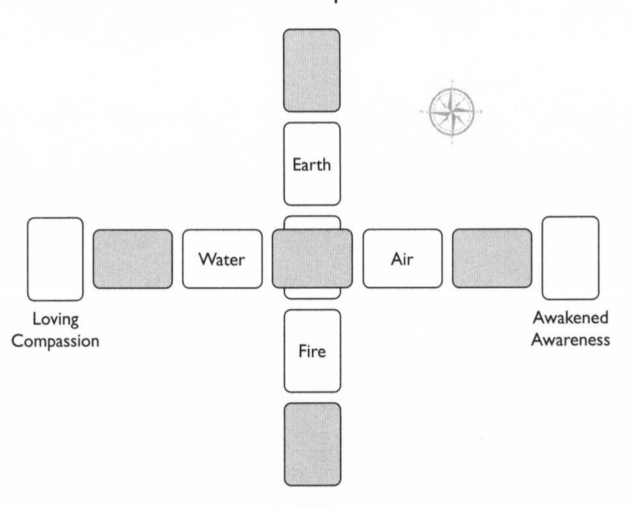

5. Turn the cards over and with the formation in front of you, draw the upward triangle/tetrahedron symbol which is located on the bottom left of the *Loving Compassion* card and the downward triangle/tetrahedron symbol from the *Awakened Awareness* card over the spread to activate the space.
6. Leave the spread set up for as long as you feel the need to.

You may wish to refer to the card meanings for insight into the themes of this layout. You can use your intuition to bridge the connection between the elemental cards and the cards you picked. However, you can simply do the layout and leave the cards to work their magic in your space.

CARD MEANINGS
Chakra Cards

1. EARTH STAR CHAKRA
Initiation

Oneness, collective consciousness, anchoring transmissions from the higher realms, sacred Earth knowledge, integration of the Divine, working with grid lines.

You are standing at a gateway into the unknown with trust in your heart, ancient remembering in your soul, and inner illumination to light the way. You have access to the seat of creation, the spark of existence, and the codes that hold the blueprints of who and what we are. This place is clear and grounded, despite moving through multidimensional realms and able to bridge worlds while functioning in physical reality. The higher you reach for the Divine and the realms of Spirit, the more important it is to anchor deeply to the Earth.

Restore: Explore clearing meditations, self-energy work and put intention into the meaningful parts of your life. Find ways to balance your life. Be aware of the times of day that are more conducive to different states of consciousness such as flow, meditation and productivity.

Themes: Integration of Spirit and the Eternal Self. How you balance spiritual and physical reality.

Healing Position: At the feet (thirty centimetres below the feet but placing the card at the feet is fine).

Colour Wash: Earth brown.

2. ROOT CHAKRA
Ground and Centre

Foundations, grounding, basic needs, survival, physical identity, responsibilities, the place where we build our lives, time in nature.

This image speaks of finding home within yourself, a sense of deep inner peace and a strong sense of grounding and being centred. Here, you can be released from the grips of survival into a place of thriving. There is trust, connection to community, and you can rely on others and joyfully understand your responsibilities in turn. You are held and have strong foundations for all aspects of life. With your guard down, you have the tools to ride the waves if you need. Everything is okay.

Restore: Spend time in nature. Sit or stand barefoot in nature and feel your roots merging with the earth beneath you. Consider your founding beliefs. If they no longer serve you, it may be time to reconsider your priorities or the foundations you live your life by. Be aware of any recurring patterns that may be holding you back.

Themes: Home, foundations, physical bases and responsibility.

Healing Position: Base of the spine, groin.

Colour Wash: Red.

3. SACRAL CHAKRA
Core of Creation

Feelings, emotional responses, pleasure, sensuality, intimacy, connection, letting go, creativity, sacred sexuality, passion, healthy boundaries, valuing the body.

You are invited to revel in the present moment and feel deeply into your senses. The sensuality of being alive, the breeze on your skin, the scent of damp earth, the feeling of fitting perfectly into the temple you call your body. This card is about diving into the depths of a moment, where all your faculties are available for divine creation. Your entire paint kit is present, as no part is left in the past or caught in the future. All of who you are unites in a point of deep experience. This is the ecstatic moment of conception for a project or new life. Let yourself drop into passion, intimacy and loving connection with whatever you are birthing into the world and with whomever you have chosen to co-create with.

Restore: Get in touch with your creativity and embrace your natural expression, however it looks to you. The way you live is an art form – a unique expression of yourself. You can dance through challenge, sing through restriction and paint your reality.

Themes: Your relationship with your body, your sensuality and your sexuality.

Healing Position: Lower abdomen, pelvis area.

Colour Wash: Vibrant orange.

4. SOLAR PLEXUS CHAKRA
Radiant Illumination

Personal power, independence, self-discipline, confidence, assertiveness, decision-making, belief, intellectual abilities, expression of will, bringing ideas into reality.

The solar plexus chakra is the radiant centre of our being. It holds the vibrant spark that brings our passions to life. Enter this space to step away from playing small, unworthiness, the idea that you are taking up space and insecurity-based competitiveness. Allow yourself to be attuned to the abundant life force that resides within this centre, and be energised, motivated, fuelled with inspiration, enthused and clear-minded, so you can bring forth more of yourself and what you wish to birth in the world. As you discover a deep and real sense of self-empowerment, you can more confidently lift others in celebration, harmonising differences and shifting hierarchical paradigms into collective co-creation.

Restore: Remember that you are a powerful being who can connect with potent life-force energy as and when you need it. Be aware of what fuels your fire and consider circumstances where you had your power away. Imagine all the fragments of your energy that you have given away at some point and bring them all back to the centre of your being.

Themes: Your power and where you are putting your energy.

Healing Position: Navel.

Colour Wash: Golden yellow.

5. HEART CHAKRA
Unfurling Back to Love

Love for oneself and others, relationships, compassion, forgiveness, empathy, connection, receptivity, acceptance, generosity.

This chakra card represents love in its many forms. It reminds you that everything in life can unfold into love or fear. When unfurled back enough, the foundation of all you seek lies in the universal desire and right to feel love and be loved. Love heals. God is love. This is the force that will change the world.

Restore: Count everything in your life that you are grateful for. Think of all those you love and how that wonderful feeling radiates from your heart. Consider those you can forgive and extend that feeling out to them. Remember, we all just want to be loved and accepted, but insecurities and triggers can cause behaviours that move us away from this place. Have compassion. Know that others may be in their suffering. Expand your awareness and heart-centred radiance for all beings on the planet – encapsulate Earth in loving compassion. Bask in the blissful feeling of the planet, in all of its perfect balance, loving you back.

Themes: Relationships and relating. Connection to yourself and others. The language of love.

Healing Position: Over the heart.

Colour Wash: Soft emerald green.

6. HIGH HEART CHAKRA
Ecstatic Bliss

Divine love, selflessness, spiritual compassion, oneness through heart-centred bliss, healing, gratitude, giving love, dharma, patience, joy.

This card taps into the blissful oneness we feel as we drop away our edges and protective containers. This is the place where we feel held and seen, enough to flow into oneness, where the eternal part of me meets the eternal part of you. This is the selfless state where our higher selves commune, for illuminated perspective on how we share, gift and lift others in our joyful overflow.

Restore: Consider your life purpose by exploring what allows you to give in joy.

Themes: The ways you can bring joy to yourself and others.

Healing Position: The thymus gland (behind your sternum, a little above the heart).

Colour Wash: Iridescent pink.

7. THROAT CHAKRA
Express Your Truth

Expression, communication, your own creative language, sharing your spirit, accepting your originality, truth, authenticity.

This chakra is the origin of expression. It is the source of the life spark that inspires our aliveness and stokes the creative fires in others. This is the outer sharing of our inner being … the glowing song of our soul, on the winds of our flight to understanding more of who we are. Connect to the crux of your potential and take it further than you could have imagined. As spirit fuses into the tangible, it actualises as a platform for greater experience and new facets are sculpted, seeded and shared as a fractal of light in the form of our own unique language.

Restore: Be truthful with yourself about how you are really feeling. If you always act in integrity and follow your heart-centred truth, some unhealthy connections or aspects of your life may fall away, and you will be in complete alignment with your path. In this way, your internal/psychic navigation system will become strengthened, your purpose will be clear, and you will inspire others through the sparkle of your deep inner knowing.

Themes: How you share your spirit. Your unique language.

Healing Position: Throat.

Colour Wash: Vibrant mid-blue.

8. THIRD EYE CHAKRA
Pineal Perspective

The seat of wisdom and consciousness, intuition, imagination, seeing inner and outer worlds, limitlessness, understanding.

Connect with your third eye and transcend what you understand with your mind. Discover a deeper inner knowing through the interconnected web of all this is and has been. You can tune into this wisdom at will, as and when you wish to. This wisdom is ancient yet pioneering. It is the creator of the free will we choose to weave from moment to moment. Be the observant witness, allow the transcendence of duality, without judgement. Be mindful, listen and allow your unfurling intuition to unravel the paradoxes of reality.

Restore: Examine limiting ideas, listen more, balance the left hemisphere's logical and analytical thinking with inner guidance and deeper wisdom. Take note of any thought patterns that may be holding you from your fullest potential, through the mind-based fear of past experiences.

Themes: Enhancing your imagination or intuition. Seeing beyond illusion.

Healing Position: Between the eyebrows.

Colour Wash: Deep indigo blue.

9. CROWN CHAKRA
The Unlimited Self

Devotion, inner guidance, visionary inspiration, fathoming beyond the mind, enlightenment, connection to the Universe and life-force energy.

The crown chakra is your link to the multidimensionality of your being. The seat of your soul, it gracefully connects you to the Heavens. The infinity symbol of limitlessness appears within the unfolding petals and points to your most potent potential. Here, you can delight in the divine strands of light that dance with us when we are aligned with spirit, purpose and truth.

Restore: Be present and flowing without rigid outcomes. Find more spaces in your life. Find your own way to meditate. When you are distracted, you are living on the surface level. Explore the state of flow and be receptive to the intuitive messages you may receive.

Themes: The way for you to be most aligned with divine guidance and connection with spirit.

Healing Position: Top of the head or just above the head if lying down.

Colour wash: White with flecks of gold and violet.

10. SOUL STAR CHAKRA
Merging with the Divine

Transcendence, letting go, being filled with divine light, channelling, karmic records, the bridge between the spiritual and the physical realms, ascension.

This image captures the merging of time beyond space and kaleidoscopic wisdom that penetrates our being. We have lived in many worlds. All interconnected, they uphold the lessons they carry as messages of transformation. Their synergy creates the expansion of the Universe. Gaze into the place where the light between our stardust can become anything, and collective evolution is part of a grander story. When we simply let go, we become all that we have been seeking and glimpse the greater dream.

Restore: Remember that you are an infinite being with the ability to expand your awareness beyond space and time. Consider that paradigms outside this physical reality may be unfathomable until we raise our vibration and can think outside the mind. Meditate on the idea that everything that ever was and ever will be is happening simultaneously, right now, across multiple dimensions.

Themes: Karma or what can be implemented or cleared for your optimal progress toward ascension.

Healing Position: Fifteen centimetres above the head. For a card healing, anywhere just above the head is fine.

Colour wash: Kaleidoscopic rainbow.

CARD MEANINGS
Elemental Cards

11. AETHER

The Seamless Unspeakable

Zero-point field, the void, blank canvas, threshold, anything is possible, time to choose what you want to bring into your life, endless possibilities, limitlessness, paradox.

This illuminated space of no distraction and pure potential is beyond the threshold. It is the silent, meditative moment out of time; the centred and present place beyond the hustle of the mind and outside world. It is where all dreams are birthed and it is the light we may fear to be darkness when, just for one moment, everything ceases to exist. This is the place between worlds, the womb before we incarnate, and from here, we can choose where we go. The land has been tilled in readiness for the flowers we wish to seed, outdated doors have been closed, and in the space between the breaths, we open the new ones.

What may be perceived as the endless, black nothingness is actually the illuminated eternal – the core that all our fears may be peeled back to. When we step though the darkness, we realise it is only a short distance away from the white void at the centre of creation and Heaven. Herein lies the feeling that we may have been striving our whole life to meet and yet simultaneously, subconsciously, running from. In this place of graceful surrender, we may know we are held and allow ourselves the spaciousness to drop deeper into the experience of our existence.

Themes: Too elusive and mysterious to define, a knowing without words, the spaces in between, life-force energy.

12. WATER
The Overflow

Abundance, non-attachment, the paradigm of no scarcity, allowing financial and energetic gifts to flow through and create more.

During one of my most pivotal Lemurian visions, I was guided into a life where I lived in a humble mud hut. As I could create any thought in the multiple dimensions that I had access to, I simultaneously resided in a beautiful crystalline palace. I found myself in a paradigm where I could create anything at will, and thus, there was no concept of scarcity nor the need to hold onto anything. This experience initiated a shift that changed my life. We may only be starting to touch on this notion in our mundane reality. When we give more from a place of overflow than obligation, even when we think we have nothing, having it come from this mindset can only create a more abundant flow of what we want.

The being in the picture has many hands and yet still, the water is allowed to fall through her fingers. It blesses her in the moments it touches her radiant skin and then continues on its journey. Her heart is also overflowing, with love. Her eyes are filled with tears. She allows what comes through to move her, without control. She gracefully allows whatever she is feeling to be expressed and as she does so, she radiates so much light into the world.

Themes: Allowing for flow, receptivity, the path of least resistance, purity, clearing away that which no longer serves, emotion.

13. AIR
Paradigm Shift

An innovative way of existing, new earth energies, inspiring others, fresh air, flying higher than you have before, more expansive perspectives, consciousness shift.

We are in a time of great change, and the speed of our evolution is increasing exponentially. With our advancing technology and ability to communicate, more knowledge and power are available to us, as individuals, than we have had for centuries. There are also more platforms where we can share this information. We have the ability to connect with the tribes who are making a difference, to connect with a web of change where our lights unite and increase. Information that was inaccessible, taboo or shrouded in mystery or initiation, especially in the healing arts, is now available. We can engage many tools as we build energetic sovereignty and create pockets where we can choose to make big changes in our communities. We can inspire others, connect the dots and receive and share the knowledge and tools needed for transformation. As we wake up, we can't help but awaken those around us. It may start with an inquiry on what this fresh, new and long-awaited breath in is all about.

An expansive being holds a tiny heart-shaped seedling. When the foundations we build on come from a place of love over fear, we will see huge positive changes in the world. We can start with ourselves.

Themes: Communication, sharing wisdom, the breath of life, movement, faith, winged helpers, intention, inspiration, change.

14. EARTH
Nurture Nature

Looking after the planet, the ebb and flow of life, the loving embrace of Mother Nature, the natural beauty of death and decay, the macro-microcosm, time in nature, ancestors, growth through weathering storms, nurturing self and heart so you may flourish.

No one can hold us the way nature can. Mama nature is a powerful healer and transmuter of dense energies we may be holding on to. Just as she takes in our out breath and returns our bones to fertile soil, so too can she transform our woes if we can allow ourselves to surrender, to lie in her grassy arms or be embraced by her branches. Just as plastics and oils cannot be broken down in the earth for renewal, when our emotions become hardened and impenetrable, catalysed into something more destructive, they cannot be transformed into the compost that we grow from. Experiences we may categorise as good or bad are a part of life. Death and rebirth are part of the natural cycle that allows for the continuation of life. Creating something through suppression and control that will not break down, will only bring us further out of harmony.

Nature is all around us. Notice her and know that when you feel like no one else can hold you, she can. Spend as much time in nature as possible and do what you can to preserve it.

Themes: Grounding, finding our roots, reliability, physical healing, nurture, solid foundations, fertility, vitality.

15. FIRE

Solerus Sublime

Duality, creation, kundalini, the rising phoenix, bringing conflict into harmony, intensity, transformation, the incredibleness of being alive, coalescence, infinite energy.

We live in a dualistic world of light and dark, yin and yang, masculine and feminine. Focusing only on light can repress our shadows. Bringing both sides into balance, and being real with our humanness, allows us to reach more joy, authenticity and depth. By accepting and loving all of ourselves as we truly are, we can extend more of this love and have deeper compassion with others.

This painting portrays the balanced dance of creation. The greater the distance of separation, of duality, the greater the density. As the dragons come together, they dissolve into one with all that is. In this place of coalescence, the fusion brings both sides together in oneness, not just as a remerging with the universe, but in an alchemical process of becoming the empowered Creator Force we truly are.

Themes: Passion, motivation, destruction, power, illumination, determination, inner light, forging forward, transformation.

16. LOVING COMPASSION

Unconditional love, empathy, compassion, care, friendliness, goodwill, benevolence, beyond duality, safe space, forgiveness through expanded perspectives, open-hearted joy.

Loving kindness is one of the greatest forces available to us on Earth. It has the ability to transform all. Unconditional love is the vibration most closely aligned with God or the Divine. When we allow ourselves to drop deep into heart-space we feel interconnected and in a state of oneness.

As we choose to direct our lives with love, all that is not real or serving us will drop away. Conflicts resolve, power struggles dissolve, and a sense of inner peace and comfort will radiate from within. Love is the root of happiness. When we can fluidly give and receive with the ease of breathing in and out, we can fly freely.

Loving compassion is a fundamental element in the balance of life. It holds the seeds of the new paradigm of evolution. When doing hands-on healing, this is the force we call on. It is life-force energy or god essence, and it brings healing, vitality and transformation to everything it touches.

When we manifest or affirm something into the world from a place of love, the reasoning imbued in the statement will reflect our intent. If we manifest from fear, our journey will bring all the learning needed to gear us back into love.

Unconditional love transcends duality. It sees beyond reasoning and situation to allow new stories to be told and for new beginnings to emerge. It transmutes all that is out of balance back to zero point and bridges heaven and earth.

Divinatory Meaning

This card invites you to bring more loving to the situation at hand, whether it is toward yourself or someone connected to the question. It may imply a need for forgiveness or for seeing things from a fresh, more expansive perspective. This card is a reminder that you are loved and have infinite access to the gentle yet powerful force of loving compassion as and when you need it. To bring yourself back into your heart, think about those you love and moments with them where you have felt joy. Expand this feeling out to more and more people, creatures and places, until the whole planet is infused with this beautiful, warm and loving feeling.

17. AWAKENED AWARENESS

Beyond the veil, clearing distortion and illusion, awareness of what's running us subconsciously, communing with our god force, energetic sovereignty, growth outside your comfort zone, the collective awakening.

Physical reality is the tip of the iceberg. The tapestry we see at surface level is just a fraction of what is going on beyond. Awakened awareness can take place when we start to look between the lines at recurring themes, aspects and symbols that gain our intuitive attention. These are keys to a hidden, overarching plan and a greater weaving. This oracle speaks to the deeper nature behind all we can know with our eyes and minds. Also known as the matrix or the veil, once discovered, it is so easy to get lost in it.

We are conditioned to be disoriented in our physical reality so that anything outside of it becomes unfathomable. Thus, we seek a framework that parallels the nature of the laws of this limiting place. And yet, there is a lot more going on, and our awakening awareness would like us to stretch our consciousness to grasp it. This awareness activates our intuitive system, helps us navigate what is true and supports us in becoming more sovereign and empowered.

We can become more ensnared in the matrix when we are lost in what is running us internally. Running away and/or distracting ourselves may offer short-term relief or band-aid our subtle but deep suffering. Society is coated with a layer of conformity. The idea of '*that's just the way things are done*' roadblocks questions when things may be out of alignment. But as we step free and awaken, we gain a more holistic approach to consciousness and come to know ourselves more deeply. We can then take things into our own hands and make changes in the world, thus regaining energy, choice and abundance that is rightfully ours. As we wriggle into the revelations of freedom, we can't help but awaken those around us.

A single glimpse of the limitless eternal and your life will never be the same again. When we directly experience the transient yet profound moment of existence, we can allow the constructs we have spent our lives believing to drop away. Our knowledge of the eternal doesn't leave us, although we may forget it. As we return to our humanness, we may use reasoning to write it off. Or, we may create whole religions around it, in an effort to grasp and recreate it.

When we look into the eyes of God, our consciousness raises, so we can fathom the unfathomable. This expansive experience can never be boxed into words or intellect, but artists, poets and musicians may be able to share, in a small way, the essence that helps us remember ourselves back into our true state. The portals into this experience are vast in number and form. For me, awakened awareness has come through deep meditation, ecstatic dance and journeying with my dharma. In essence, connecting with this element is about raising our vibration, getting out of our heads and allowing our spirit to lead the way.

When we walk behind the veil, we discover our true path. Our reason for being here is revealed in symbolic jigsaw-puzzle pieces and synchronicities. The mysteries unweave, and the paradoxes speak to a different part of us. Our affirmations are potent, our prayers are heard and the medicine of life lessons, however strong and uncomfortable, is full of powerful growth.

This is one of the elemental cards because without moment-to-moment awakened awareness, magic, healing and affirmation cannot be deep or real way enough to actualise. This not just imagining God, but seeing, knowing and communing with the divine spark inside each of us.

Divinatory Meaning

This card is a reminder to wake up! There are many levels and stages of awakening. There is no on/off switch. Keep learning and putting yourself into situations where you can grow. Sometimes we do go back to sleep, so stay aligned with your inner guidance and find ways to remember to wake up.

Do what you love to keep your vibe high. This is not about instant pleasure, but the joy that is substantial and sustainable. Eat healthily, keep your body active, and have life goals but with enough space to hear the answers to your prayers.

When our energy systems become blocked or need a cleanse, we can become drowsy to our vital nature. Energy clearing can help you re-centre. Shadow work may also be needed if certain things are running your mind in a disempowering and distorting way.

Find your unique way to connect to the Divine inside you – not as an external seeking but as a receptive allowing. Be inspired to see the question at hand with a different perspective. Look between the lines for a deeper interpretation.

CARD MEANINGS
Seed Cards

18. ALIGNMENT

Inner integrity, being a vibrational match for what you want to bring into your life, manifesting from a place of love over fear, energy flows where attention goes, subconscious sabotage, seamlessly actualising our dreams.

We all have the ability to manifest the life we wish to call in. However, we may find our desires are not actualising as we hoped. Energy goes where attention flows, and if our thoughts and focus fixate on something that opposes what we want to bring to our lives, this will cause dissonance. Is there an internal sabotage? Are we, without realising, undermining ourselves through our language, our worries, and the broken records that play in our minds?

To bring something to your life, become the vibrational match for it. Imagine what it feels like to already have what you desire and cultivate that feeling. This is the key to powerful manifesting. Preparing ourselves and our environment, as if what we are manifesting is a certainty also creates a shift in our thinking. When we want and strive for something, we create more wanting and striving. When we immerse ourselves in what it is like to already have something, we will be in the perfect vibration to receive it.

Also, consider whether you are choosing to manifest something from fear or love. Unfortunately, if our wants are driven by or born out of fear, we will amplify this. When our heart motivates our desires, whatever we manifest is aligned with love.

Divinatory Meaning

Look at where your desires and manifestations are being seeded. If your plans or dreams aren't unfolding as you would like them to, it's time to take a deeper look at other areas in your life. Is something out of step with integrity? Are you making decisions through fear or love? If it is through fear or avoidance, your manifestations may seemingly backfire to encourage experiences that will bring you back into balance. It is time to become a vibrational match for what you are seeking. Instead of striving harder for something, cultivate the feeling of already having all you seek. You will be surprised at what this shift in perspective creates.

19. BALANCED FORCES

Yin and Yang, productive flow, masculine and feminine energy, the balance of duality, patriarchal paradigm being re-balanced, equality, balance in perspective.

The Lemurian people are said to have been androgynous, meaning they were not a specific gender. As they were only partially formed in the physical realm, they did not inhabit a paradigm of duality. They were a perfect balance of what became masculine and feminine energy as it densified in physical form.

We all hold a mix of masculine and feminine energies within us. Masculine energy is more about focus in a forward direction, while feminine energy is more holistic and peripheral. Masculine energy is that of logistics and actioning desires into being, and it has more of a controlled and rigid vibration. Feminine energy is freer flowing, nurturing, creative and receptive. Both sides are to be celebrated but, in our efforts to rebalance, inequality and prejudice can occur.

In the current paradigm, masculine and feminine energies are imbalanced as our global culture is largely patriarchal and strongly influenced by masculine energy. Efforts to revitalise the feminine flow have been incrementally shifting the balance over the last century. It is time to calm mind-based intellect, scientific data, linear direction and the acquisition of power.

To have an optimal human experience, we must embody a balance of masculine and feminine energies. We can daydream in receptive fluidity, and then action our ideas into reality. We can be soft and nurturing and also firm and direct as needed.

We can be determined, compassionate, grateful, vulnerable, visionary and strong. There can be focus and free flow. We may not draw on these energies simultaneously, but when we access both equally we can be truly powerful centred beings. When we bridge the duality within ourselves, we can seed more balance in our outer world.

Divinatory Meaning

This card invites you to look at masculine and feminine energy from a more balanced perspective. Is the situation at hand on the more masculine side of the spectrum? Can it be tempered with feminine energy? Vice versa, would the addition of masculine energy bring balance? What needs to happen to form a more holistic and equalised foundation? Do you normally hold a position of one extreme? How might you balance this so you can experience a more optimised state of being? To bring more masculine drive and focus to a situation (for instance, if you have some upcoming due dates and you need to get into action mode) focus on your goals, desires and ambitions. If you want to engage more feminine energy, for receptivity, trust, flow and surrender, consider all the things you are grateful for already. Feel the warmth, gratitude and comfort of knowing everything is divinely perfect just the way it is.

20. BEYOND THE MIND

Thinking with the heart, being present, heart and mind connection, meditation, the bliss of being, quieting the monkey mind, fathoming the unfathomable, finding happiness within, going beyond intellectual limitation.

The mind is a wonderful tool for moving us through the logistical elements of life so we can function in the world. However, its endless chatter, self-doubt, limiting stories and subconscious programs can also keep us in our suffering. One of the fundamental problems with mind chatter is that it takes us out of the present moment. As soon as we are in the past or future, we can no longer be our most empowered in the present.

When we are stuck in the past or worrying about our future, we are not in command of our *now*. All we are doing is draining our energy and removing ourselves from the beauty of this incredible moment where anything is possible. That is not to say we shouldn't plan for the future or honour the past. This message is about bringing our awareness to the present.

We are naturally wired to be everywhere but the present moment. Just as we would exercise to keep our body fit and healthy, it is useful to practise being here and now. Learning to find inner spaces of peace and silence, regardless of external circumstances, is one of the greatest gifts we can cultivate for ourselves.

Much of Western culture and society pivots on a mind-based paradigm. This has served us in getting from A to B in a very linear way, but it is not holistic, and the cracks are starting to show. We learn that logic is always the right approach. However, more and more people are feeling unfulfilled, unhappy and anxious, even though we are living more comfortably and with fewer threats.

What can we do about this? The answer is learning to just be – even just for ten minutes of your day. There are many techniques to help you to quieten the mind. Find the ones that work for you and as your internal world becomes more peaceful, conscious, empowered and meaningful, so too will your external world. They are interconnected.

True bliss is experienced completely and utterly in the present moment. In essence, it is the feeling we spend so much of our life seeking. Ironically, we have access to this feeling always, without external stimulants or concepts. Allow everything to drop away, so you are present. It can take some work, but presence and bliss are totally within your grasp.

Commodity-driven society tells us we need to seek things outside of ourselves to feel safe and happy. This thinking keeps us out of the magic! The enlightened soul knows there is so much more.

Divinatory Meaning

Take a step outside your mind-based concerns or limitations. Looking at things in an overly logical way will hinder you and obstruct access to your superpowers. You may be transfixed by a past experience. The past may be running you and making your mind spin so you cannot see what is really in front of you. Consider what your heart and your gut are telling you. Step back and clear your mind. Meditate in your own way. Contemplate what the situation at hand would feel like if you released all fears and worries. Are these concerns even yours?

21. COMMUNICATION CO-CREATION

Non-verbal communication, love language, telepathy, unique ways of communication, light language, multidimensional information, community coexistence, relationships, meeting our higher selves, really 'seeing' someone, deeper listening.

We normally think of information as something that can be written or spoken, but if something is multidimensional, it is almost impossible to share it with words. I feel I have quite a lot of this information in my field now, and yet my intelligence cannot fathom it. Metaphor or song may hint at its vastness, but it is more like a reminder or catalyst that encourages something to stir inside the listener.

Art is one way I have sought to share this information. Whatever language you speak, the emotion and message of art and music can be understood. In my healing work, where I feel the energy that comes through hands, there is a sense that my soul and that of the client are in deep conversation. I often feel that I am much more competent at conversation in these realms. My synaesthesia allows me to navigate this information in real-time rather than having to slow down and translate it into words that feel constricting and dull compared to the vast yet simple nature of what I am looking to express. This is why I paint. A lot of the work I do is in the unseen realm, but I understand part of my role is to bridge these realities and inspire a wider understanding of what is possible.

Thus, you may notice unusual looking codes in many of

my paintings. I have experienced many visual downloads of luminescent coding that can be simple figures or complex and large enough to step into for an activation or healing transmission. The download experience is extremely blissful, visual, and with a sense of fathoming the unfathomable. When I return to my normal state of being, the information no longer makes sense. People often ask about the codes in my paintings. I ask them to imagine a whole library's worth of information imbued in a single letter, then extending that to encompass a whole sentence. The codes can open us to all that the multidimensional worlds can share. They are portals to the edges of our conceivable realities. I have come to understand the codes are *light language* and have revelled in meeting other visionary artists who have painted almost identical light codes.

As we evolve our conscious awareness, we start to pick up on information, such as what those around us are about to say, or that which the universe is trying to tell us.

Divinatory Meaning

How are you communicating beyond words? Perhaps you are being misunderstood because there is a dissonance between your words, actions and behaviour, and what you mean to communicate. Words are like spells, so be conscious of what you say as you may be verbally sabotaging your intended meaning. Also, be reminded that words can mean different things to different people. Something may be getting lost in translation. An issue may be cleared through improved communication. Listen carefully to what someone has to say, without interruption. Furthermore, it may feel scary to share vulnerable truths, but this may be the only way forward. This card also encourages greater exploration in the realms of telepathy, healing and the arts such as poetry, painting and music, where there is collective communication beyond the mind.

22. CRYSTAL KEYS

Hidden wisdom codes, potent information, Lemurian seed crystals, seeing your triggers as a gift, awareness of drama-creating patterns, healing the earth by looking at your inner environment, healing through awareness.

Lemurian quartz crystals are special pieces of clear quartz with indented ridges running across them. They are known as *seed crystals* because they are said to have been found individually, buried in sand and earth, rather than attached to a larger cluster the way most crystals are. Aware of their oncoming destruction, the Lemurians imbued information about how to avoid a similar catastrophe on crystals and buried them. The ridges on the crystals are believed to be Lemurian inscriptions. These crystals are reappearing now as this knowledge is again relevant.

This card is about deciphering wisdom codes. We may wonder how to access information regarding our spiritual growth as we navigate our everyday reality. This wisdom comes through inner paradoxes, when we are truly present, awed, in creative flow or a state of surrender. It may come as riddles and in the most unlikely places. Zen Buddhism taps into this using koans, paradoxical statements the mind cannot fathom, to bypass traditional understanding and allow spiritual epiphany and a deeper knowledge of the soul to surface.

Key wisdom codes can come to us when we are triggered. They are accessible in those moments when everything becomes more emotional, dramatic or painful than it needs to be. Here, when light shines on our shadow, we are graced with significant insight into places we can grow and evolve from, although it might take courage and a healthy dose of self-awareness to embrace the wisdom of those moments. It's amazing how much energy, freedom and expansion comes as a result of deciphering these bubbles of information, tailored especially for us. Sometimes insight is so perfectly constructed within a scenario that it gets right into our most tender spots for the perfect healing.

These are potent codes as all personal power struggles and ego problems affect the bigger picture of how the world operates. Our shadows are unresolved wisdom codes. Avoidance makes them spiral out to aid in the construction of a world we don't actually want, both individually and collectively. When we see this information as the gift that it is, we can cultivate presence and begin to see between the lines of our inner workings. The world needs as much light as possible, so we do not have a repeat of what happened in Lemuria. Let's allow ourselves to see our shadows as an opportunity to bring more light into our being and heal the world from these dark foundations.

Divinatory Meaning

Be inspired to find the wisdom hidden in those times when you feel triggered. There is so much information within our raw and intense reactions that when you choose to be present with what is coming up and peel back the layers, great spiritual insight will unveil itself in a way tailored just for you. If we could all learn to see our triggers in the bigger picture, so much confrontation and upset would be lessened, power struggles and fear would diminish, and we would see greater compassion across the planet. Perspective and misunderstanding would shift, and the way people want to be loved would be experienced without distortion. These are the seeds for peace on Earth.

23. ENDLESS OPPORTUNITIES

Decision-making, choice, crossroads, unrealised opportunities, taking the path of least resistance, heart over mind, direction, focused energy, the high road or the low road.

Decisions, decisions, options and opportunities. It's wonderful that we have the freedom to choose. But, times of indecision can be so hard and almost suffocating. The more we use our minds to battle the pros and cons, the more we move out of our hearts. Often the best way forward is to step back and do what it takes to get out of your head and into your body so your 'gut feeling' can guide the way.

When making a choice, you may consider anything that doesn't feel like a total yes as a total no. Perhaps none of the apparent options are right? Or, any choice could be the right one, if you wholeheartedly pick a direction and give it your best shot. When faced with a decision, check where your integrity lies. Peel back the layers to see where you are making your choices from. Are you choosing from fear-based survival or a place of love?

A choice founded in love can make you feel light, excited, passionate and give you butterflies. It might be a little scary, but in a good way. It might not make sense to your mind. It may seem out of your comfort zone or undermine logic. The low road can look like the safest, easiest path. It may avoid or lessen immediate pain and confrontation, but it will be long, winding and exhausting. The high road might look perturbing, but it will cut through old stories and lead directly to the heart for growth and transformation.

When you choose to step forward boldly, it takes courage, but you will discover a place of trust. Rather than staying small, hiding or running away, you will expand and open yourself to growth. This is where magic happens and synchronicities you could never have imagined land in your lap. But first, you have to step into the unknown and let your heart guide you.

What if everything you wanted was right there in front of you? Make the important decision to let go of outdated limitations. What could be the worst that happens? Reach for what you want and know it is closer than you realise.

Divinatory Meaning

You have options and opportunities you may not have realised. The Universe wants to give you what you want. It's all there, so reach out and wholeheartedly choose it. While you sit on the fence, your experiences are diluted or confusing. We live in a time of choices. Sometimes reason and limitation direct are choices, and we feel unfulfilled as a result. Choose life from a place of heart, compassion, and integrity, and you can't go wrong.

24. EVOLUTION

Growth, overcoming challenges, gracefully riding the waves of life, expanding out of a problem, flourishing in the face of change, thriving in new environments, being unperturbed.

What does personal evolution mean to you? Is it about growth, expansion, adaptation, success, or becoming a better version of yourself? Perhaps it speaks to an ability to move through difficulties? However good we are at surfing the waves of life, we all face surging tides of challenging ups and downs at times. When we try to hide from our trials, they get even bigger or more overwhelming. We can dive into them or surf them for growth and transformation. We might also flow with the current of least resistance, allowing the waves to wash over us and inspire a deeper sense of compassion and strength. How we meet our challenges contributes to our growth and evolution.

We rarely know how many 'fails' went into someone's success. Do your best, be aware that 'success' is rarely instant. It may take years of persistence. The idea that a project, quest or realisation should come together quickly and perfectly can freeze creativity. Life is about the process. Success is about perseverance.

That is not to say we should keep pushing uphill if we are not feeling it. Obligation does not have the passion and determination to press through challenges. The notion that love will find a way is relevant as challenges are more likely to be surmounted when you have the spark of passion and enjoyment in your heart. So consider what drives your bigger-picture plans and what inspired you to take this path, to chase this dream. Success is linked to doing what you love. It takes time to get good at something. When you love what you are doing you keep going, through the failures and disappointments, until you meet success.

There are challenges we have no power or control over. In those circumstances, our evolution is more of an internal process. How can we strive to see the silver lining? Find the gratitude, the learnings, and do what you feel you need to do to be real and honest with your feelings. Evolution or life-mastery is attempting every wave with courage, grace and poise. It is about meeting challenges, learning to glide across the emotionally charged waters of life and bringing joy, humour and light-heartedness along as you weave your light in the world.

Divinatory Meaning

Look for ways that you can flourish in the face of challenge. Tap into your original passion and remember why you chose the path that brought you to where you are now. Break a problem down to its elements and be creative in how you tackle them. Consider how you can make it more fun and inspiring. Alternatively, be present and ask how you can learn, grow and become stronger through what is happening for you.

Focus on the aspects of your situation that make it all worth it. Draw on the inner resources that can pull you through. You have the qualities you need to shine, so don't lose sight of the bigger picture. You may be pushed to greater and deeper learnings, and it might be an uncomfortable process, but the strength, growth and wisdom that come from journeying through the eye of the storm and embodying this knowledge is something no teacher can show you.

25. FREEDOM

Living the life you love, liberation as a shift in perspective, the many facets of freedom, inviting enjoyment and inspiration to your life, discovering what freedom means to you, overcoming limitation, unbound creative expression, choice over obligation.

Freedom means living as you choose, with your wings and heart open, able to direct your reality as you want. The quest for freedom, in one form or another, seems innate. In Western culture, the path to freedom is often equated with money. Ironically, chasing wealth can have the opposite effect due to the lengths taken for it to be acquired. It is possible to weave a life in thriving alignment with our soul's calling while financially supporting our realities.

You may picture freedom in its more extreme guises, but when we truly feel free, our lifestyles may not change drastically. It is more of a state of mind. The only change might be that you are choosing to live a certain way, rather than feeling obligated. We may move through periods of life in a dazed blur of routine. What seemed like the dream career or lifestyle may have become somewhat of a prison. We may feel stuck, blocked or uninspired. We might know deep down that it's time to step into something different but feel tied to what we have set up for ourselves, perhaps financially or because others depend on us. It may feel like something needs to change externally before you can make the step, but it doesn't usually work that way. As scary as it may seem, to get off a self-perpetuating spiral we need to initiate our own change.

Small changes that don't impinge on your work or family can be enough to tell the Universe you are ready for something else. Think about where you might find inspiration, then begin researching and try it out. Try a few new things. This will help shift the direction of your inner being. Before you know it, opportunities will start to open for you. It will then be your choice to follow a new path or to continue as you are.

Letting go, trusting and loving without limitation are also a big part of internal freedom. There are lots of ideas about what freedom can be. Having a framework for what it can be, means even more freedom can flourish. Complete freedom can also be overwhelming, confusing or ungrounding. Structure and security are friends of freedom. They support fun, safety, expansion, sustainability and exciting possibility.

Divinatory Meaning

Bring a deeper sense of freedom to a situation. A limitation may be a state of mind. A shift of perspective can help bring a sense of lightness and choice. Also consider what freedom looks like to you, in the bigger picture of your life. If you are feeling stifled in an environment, it is up to you to make a change. Add pleasurable moments or practices that cultivate a sense of greatened freedom in your day-to-day life.

If you are currently experiencing greater freedom, you may be feeling unsettled. Consider whether it is the kind you were looking for. If you feel ungrounded and lost, perhaps you could add some structure to your world to optimise your freedom.

26. FULL SPECTRUM

Creating heaven on earth by honouring the perfection of nature's cycles, going beyond the judgement of good and bad, the merging of duality, raw nature, earth wisdom, connecting to ancestors, shadows as the fertile soil for exponential growth, the way forward is in the whisperings of the land, honouring the full spectrum of life.

What does heaven on earth look like to you? Do you imagine lush green nature, ancient forests, pristine beaches, crystalline water systems and all the planet's residents in full health, living in harmony with each other? And yet, nature in its purest rawest form is a balance of life and death, growth and decomposition, the eaters and the eaten — in one way or another, this is the natural flux of life.

We already live in Eden, but our efforts to own and segregate bring us further away from this paradigm. Power trips, the need for imagined security, fear or avoidance of the shadow, keep us out of our freedom. The need to preserve and hold on tightly, only stunts our growth and leaves us drowning in a sea of plastic. The real disease on Earth, the barrier to Eden, is in our minds. Life happens, but it is our perception of good and bad and our black and white judgements that prevent us from seeing the grander truth. When duality becomes one, we will find Shamballa before us. Perhaps we can find inspiration from nature and the animal kingdom.

Does the tiny frog spend its days anxious over its vulnerable future? What happens when we realise fertile compost greets us when we allow ourselves to transmute our pain? When we honour all that came before, our roots are nourished, and we grow with more vitality, vibrancy and life force. We can anchor more light for the collective, and in turn, seed new growth.

What happens when we realise the keys to our future are in the wisdom of the earth and the dreamings of the indigenous? That the answers are in the geometry of the macro and microcosm, the nurturing embrace of oneness, in Mama Nature's arms? What happens when we find peace within the full spectrum of life?

Even the notion of separation, this *disease,* can be symbolised as no more than a blackened leaf on a healthy tree. The ebb and flow of our evolution and devolution is a temporary blip in the universe. The message is to be what we can, to ground heaven on earth, but not out of fear. We often try to avoid or run from 'negative' situations, but when fear steers our decisions and actions far more devastation can result. When we choose to let our hearts lead us away from stories and outdated patterns, our challenges become the fertile compost that feeds our ascending tendrils as they reach to the heavens and ground its light back on Earth.

Divinatory Meaning

Step out of the black-and-white mentality of judgement. Go beyond the concepts of good and bad. This card invites you to honour the full spectrum of life and find a new way of perceiving your situation. When we judge something, we create a story around it. These stories often create limitation. Subconsciously, we gather so many of these stories over a lifetime. To heal our dis-ease and crystallise the new way, we need to create a space of no story where miraculous healing can happen. This space empowers us to be all we are and allows us to know our truth.

Embrace the full spectrum of creation in all her colours, and the raw, muddy, earthbound shadow parts of a situation, to determine whether they are actually bad or if stories you have held onto are limiting your perspective.

27. FURRED & FEATHERED FRIENDS

Ethical consumption, making a difference through our food choices, caring for all beings, animals, environmental awareness, doing the best we can, animal spirit guides.

Animals are intuitive and sacred beings that walk the earth beside us. They are the wisdom keepers of many earth traditions and some of our most loving companions. They have much to teach us, and yet, the way some species are treated is quite unbelievable. As we become more empathic and our sense of compassion expands beyond that of our own family and community sphere, we start to see other beings and the quality of their lives as interconnected and equal. We may be inspired to align our actions with our compassion to minimise the harm we do to the planet and all her inhabitants.

As humans are evolving and moving to a lighter consciousness, our bodies may struggle to digest what was once healthy and fortifying. Also, when we are doing the work spiritually, we may feel more sensitive to things that don't fit with our values. When we take on the energy of a product that has suffering imbued in it, no matter how good it tastes or even how organic it is, we may notice a lowering of our vibration as it challenges our spiritual integrity.

That is not to say that there is one way of living and eating that everyone should adopt. This message is about doing the best we can within our circumstances. It is not always possible to access nutritious or locally produced alternatives. However, as consumers, we do have the power to push for change by choosing how and where we spend our money. We have many more options in the West than in previous generations for plant-based alternatives. Furthermore, there is evidence to show that minimising the intake of animal-based foods helps to address a range of endemic health issues.

As the false food pyramids fall away, they reveal themselves as misinformative, marketing tools of the meat industry. We can let go of this falsehood, and choose nourishment that is sustainable, healthy and inspiring. Also, be aware of environmental factors, such as land clearing and water use. Once you start to scratch the surface, you will discover alarming and eye-opening truths about food production. There is no need to be dogmatic about making a shift but do what you can – it does make a difference.

'May all beings everywhere be happy and free, and may the thoughts words and actions of my own life contribute in some way to that happiness and to that freedom for all.'

—Translation of the Sanskrit prayer,
Lokah Samastah Sukhino Bhavantu

Divinatory Meaning

Look at how you choose to nourish your physical body and your ethics and reasoning surrounding your food choices. Where possible, explore fortifying, filling and nourishing alternatives. Your body and energy will thank you for it. This card also signifies strong animal energies. That could mean working more closely with an animal spirit guide or bringing a four-legged companion into your life. You may have a greater awareness of the wisdom of the animals that you encounter and what their traits or messages mean to you.

28. GRACIOUS RECEPTIVITY

Gratitude, being thankful, receptivity, giving without expectation, how worthiness and self-love can affect your capacity to receive and to give without depletion, overflow over obligation, thriving over surviving, gifting economies.

If there was a manual for optimal human experience, one of the most potent points would be gratitude. It is the backbone of all spiritual practice. Writing a list of the things you are grateful for has been scientifically proven to have a profound positive effect on the mind and nervous system.

When we shift our perspective from what we are lacking, needing and desiring, we temporarily replace the survival factor with the resonance for thriving. When we acknowledge the miracle of our existence and how far we have come despite the challenges, it can bring back our inner smile. Gratitude can enliven an attitude of 'I've got this.'

One of the best tricks for bringing something into your life is to be already thankful for it – as if it has already arrived. This sets up the frequency of fullness and plenty, rather than emptiness and need. As we have mentioned before like attracts like, but there is a whole other power at play here as true gratitude is anchored in the heart. Being moved by the sheer awe of appreciation and thankfulness is hugely pivotal to the way others and our environment responds to us.

The next step is to give from our hearts without being asked or invited.When we emanate a field of new earth consciousness, giving can free us from expectation, just by knowing that we can all thrive together when everything flows as a system of gifting. (*Burning Man Festival* is a blueprint of this).

Yes, others may take advantage, but if you drop the fear of this outcome, it is quite likely that those of this frequency will also fall away. Holding up a beacon of light this way creates incentive and inspiration to those around you. As their cup fills, it unlocks space within them for resources in other areas. Thus, this giving overflow has a domino effect from person to person.

Receptivity is a critical factor in the art of giving. Those who struggle to feel they have the resources to give may also have trouble receiving. Some do not feel worthy enough to receive – even from themselves. As mentioned, heart energy is key to gratitude and receptivity. Here, it brings us to self-love and how important it is for feeling 'full enough' so that our overflow that doesn't deplete.

When you allow yourself to receive from those in their heart's joyous overflow and give from a place beyond expectation or obligation, a whole new paradigm reveals itself. You will discover a new way of thriving. Giving and receptivity is a two-way flow. Each allows space for the other. When we are in our hearts, we have limitless resources, and that starts with gratitude. Could gifting economies be the seed for a more joyful new paradigm of making the world go round?

Divinatory Meaning

Consider your relationship with gratitude, how comfortable you feel receiving, and what you love to give. Are there themes that allow you the joyous overflow of giving without limitation? How can you add this to the lives of others more often, away from the fear that you will get 'used' up if you give without guaranteed reciprocity? Are there areas where you are overextending yourself? Can you give more from areas where you are stronger and have more skill and capacity?

Right now, you may feel you have little to give. If so, allow yourself to receive more. The gift of the sun on your face on a winter's day or a compliment from a stranger – allow yourself to drink every drop. After all, it is up to you how deeply you wish to drink of the gift that is shared. Often, we take only a little sip even when there is so much more we could appreciate. And yet, it is beautiful when you give to someone, and they light up and receive it fully. Gratitude, self-love and self-worth are interwoven with the capacity to receive. Together, they nourish your soul. Step into your heart space by listing all you are grateful for and notice how full you start to feel. From this place, your gifting capacity can spiral upward.

29. HARMONIC FLIGHT

Seeing the Divine in the eyes of another, relationships with deep bonds, karmic connection, clearing illusory projections, life-changing connection, transmuting dissonance, removing heart armour, being 'seen', teamwork.

This powerful image represents the Divine we see when we look deeply into the eyes of another and our armour drops — when we meet another being, present in the moment, with no stories, judgements or insecurities. I felt a little overwhelmed and intimidated when I painted this card. I wasn't quite ready or didn't fully fathom the message. Then, some months later, I experienced it when I was looking into the eyes of my beloved. Shortly after, I encountered the Divine in the eyes of a stranger when space was held for this surrendered openness.

When we see the person standing before us as the gods and goddesses they are, it is a reminder that we are what we perceive in others. But also, when we drop into the mindless space of pure essence we might see the world seeing us seeing them seeing the infinite eternal allowing all that is.

Many people are seeking their twin flame. As life-changing, world-rocking and unfathomably beautiful finding this soul can be, it is quite possibly one of the most intensely confronting, trigger-provoking and, sometimes, painful connections we can have. Those who are most dear to us can bring us to our greatest growth. That is why spending extended periods with our family can be challenging.

When we can see and be seen, disarmoured and trusting,

we can come to deeper love. However, this deepening process can trigger the release of outdated and unhealthy patterns. Thus, shadows may be brought to the surface to heal. When we feel safe in the arms of our beloved, our defences yield so we fall further into our hearts. However, fear-based reflections or projections can surface in this place of deep vulnerability. Subconscious behaviours, including childhood patterning, can also present themselves.

It can seem as if our partner is provoking difficulties, bringing things up, and making it feel like our whole world is about to fall apart. At this point, we may want to retreat, but if we can be truly present, our fears can fall away, and this becomes an expansive experience.

When we have a profound, twin-flame connection, that feels beyond worlds and lifetimes, we bond with the other person so strongly that we choose to face the fire when we would usually walk away. Our passion drives us to seek resolution, to heal ourselves, to overcome barriers, no matter how confronting it may seem … because our partnership is worth it. And, when we can rise, we rise together.

Somehow, incredibly, the universe seamlessly aligns the places the twin flames need healing. Their triggers may be synchronised so that when they feel uncentered, or there is co-dependence or imbalance, it can be a very volatile space. If they find safety in love, and they are willing to see and be seen, their triggers can blossom into deep transformative healing for them both. This healing can forge the foundations for long-term companionship. Alternatively, this completion could mark an ending. As the intense potency of a connection neutralises, the relationship may transform into a different kind of unconditional love.

Harmonic Flight shows us that when we harmonise our

energies with that of another, in any form of relationship, we can soar to the sky. We can guide each other higher and higher, by encouraging all that has been weighing us down to drop away.

Divinatory Meaning

What you see in the eyes of another is a reflection of yourself. This card may be encouraging you to look at the bigger picture of a close relationship. A perceived challenge may be an illusion or projection. This card may relate to family, teamwork, community and ways you can harmonise dissonance for deeper growth. The bonds you share give you the power to transmute your fears. Put time and awareness into resolving karmic connections, or they will continue to play out. There may also be a life-changing connection on the horizon.

30. HEALING

Energy re-balance, energetic awareness, healing yourself and others, exploring healing modalities, Reiki, the chakra system, your unique and innate ability to heal, colour vibration, soul sovereignty, auras and the meridian system, aligning to the highest good and optimal health.

The Lemurians were well-versed in the practice of the healing arts. They were naturally intuitive and accustomed to navigating energetic-based realities. We all have natural healing abilities that are advanced when we deepen our energetic awareness. When we perceive the world beyond our more well-known senses, we start to receive information and wisdom that is different from that which stems from intellect. By tapping into life-force consciousness, and using this abounding energy alongside focused intention, we find that anything is possible.

You may already practice a form of natural healing, but find you sometimes feel quite drained. If this is the case, ensure the energy you are overflowing comes from an infinite stream of abundant universal energy. Rather than using your own resources, you may want to imagine the brightest, most love-imbued luminescent light, flowing down from the heavens or the centre of the Universe. And, alongside any healing intentions, include the statement, "For the greatest good."

Many healing modalities work with high vibrational energies. It can be wonderful to explore these in conjunction with your current practices. If you haven't done healing work before but feel called to do so now, follow this instinct. Being able to offer healing to loved ones or yourself is a gift. Exploring the art of energetic healing will significantly increase your psychic sensitivity.

Energetic healing is based on the meridian systems of the body. These systems, the chakras, are often depicted as coloured wheels of light. Each chakra connects to organs of the body, emotions and related characteristics. Emanating from these powerful vortices is the energy field known as the aura. It is possible to train yourself to see the electromagnetic field around the body, and it can be photographed. The appearance of the aura is influenced by the chakras. Muddier or darker colours in the aura might imply some 'spring cleaning' is in order (For more on this see text for *The Violet Flame*).

Colour is how we perceive light frequencies. Every colour has a different vibration. Crystals are formed through vibration, and each carries its own frequency. Crystals are often used in spiritual healing because they hold the frequencies to bring the chakra points into balance. Sound healing is another example of this. Immersion in a sound bath experience aligns the brainwaves with frequencies conducive to self-healing as well as body and energy wholeness. We feel, hear and receive the sounds and are organically aligned to the same frequency they resonate at.

Many tools can help us restore our centred state of balance and our access to life-force power. When we engage them, the benefits will flow on to others. Healing is a path to true empowerment and energetic sovereignty. As we collectively raise our vibrations and wake each other up, we will see massive shifts forward, and old hierarchal foundations will fall away.

Divinatory Meaning

Extend the margins of your awareness. Revisit the situation in question from a broader perspective or higher vibration with a focus on healing. This will help you decipher what is real, possible ways forward, and whether an issue is really a problem at all. This card can also signify the universal push that inspires you to explore your healing abilities, however that looks to you.

31. HOME

Heart-based presence, grounding, finding home within yourself wherever you are, the body as a temple for the soul, travel, finding family wherever you go, occupying yourself, connecting to your unwavering infinite depths and the collective oneness.

This painting has journeyed with me, under my arm, for many nomadic excursions. It is a serendipitous reminder to find my way back to the heart within my divine inner universe. Revelling in the outer exploration of this magnificent Earth has often left me unrooted and ungrounded, and this provoked my curiosity for what 'home' feels like. The notion of 'home as where the heart is' unravelled and reshaped as I realised it is any place where the vibration and resonance are clearly aligned with you. Your outer world is a reflection of your inner world. However, your environment – the place and the people – also affects your energy.

The title of this painting is *Home*, also known as *heart-shaped portal outside of the matrix*. Our way home, to oneness and the truest part of our infinite selves, is to know ourselves beyond the socialised matrix of mind-constructed reality. Deep heart-based presence is a direct portal home.

What does 'home' feel like to you? Do you feel at home in your body? Does it feel like a safe space to rest your soul? Are there unloved parts of yourself? Do you ever really feel quite right? What is your relationship with your body?

Not being fully in our bodies, is referred to as being

ungrounded or uncentered. When our thoughts are a few steps ahead or behind, so follows our consciousness. When all sense of flighty survival drops away, a deep sigh radiates from the safe space within. You hold the environment, the platform, where you can ground dreams into realities. When you come home to this place, you will know a blissful presence and a warm inner glow of unconditional love. Wherever you go, you will feel a sense of home, and whoever you encounter, you will meet as family.

Divinatory Meaning

This card invites you to align with your temple space. Consider all the amazing things your body does and how you effortlessly move through reality. Become aware of the many gifts that come from a deep sense of truly occupying your 'self'. Often, very intuitive souls exist within the upper chakras and may struggle with the density of 'human-ing'. You may not feel like you are from here, but as though you are more accustomed to navigating a world with different parameters. At this time on Earth, it is a blessing to have the vessel of a body. It is an opportunity to make a difference, so celebrate it! You have dreams and visions and may yearn to float around in more etheric realms, but it is when we are fully grounded and present in our bodies that we can actualise these ideas and make a difference. Be grounded, find your home, as just like a tree, the deeper our roots, the higher we can reach into the heavens.

32. INTERNAL EXPLORER

Flow-state, accessing infinite information by going within, wisdom from the collective consciousness, theta waves, channelling, breaking free from limiting intellect, creative boldness, being guided by the divine spark, you already hold the keys.

When we stop looking outside ourselves and surrender to a soft inner focus, we have access to unlimited information and resources. When we stop thinking with the glass ceiling of our intellect, we have access to multidimensional wisdom from the collective consciousness. Have you ever felt in total flow? Perhaps when speaking about something profound, that you have total faith in, you have heard your words articulately unfold? At other times, when you have doubt, you must watch your words, and they come out disjointed, only hinting at what you are trying to say.

In my journey as an artist, I found I was able to paint more skilfully than I imagined when I stopped thinking or tightly controlling my images into being. This was especially so when I was starting out. By getting out of my own way, I could get into a flow that felt like something else was guiding my paintbrush. This is known as 'flow-state' and is said to be the optimal state for higher function.

When in deep flow-state, it can seem as if something else is guiding me. Perhaps it is my higher self? People often ask whether I have a strong concept of what I will paint before I start. I do have a half-formed idea, but the state I find myself in when I paint allows the rest of the image to form itself. I don't try to control it too much. When I allow myself to really go there and listen to the whispers that guide the journey, it gives more 'soul' to my pieces. These are the creations that people most resonate with – the ones that prompt a mysterious sense of 'remembering'.

I am dyslexic and do not think of myself as an author, so the prospect of writing the text for this guidebook could have been quite overwhelming. But, I was guided to drop into the vibration of the card and trust that the words would flow. I reached a deeper part of myself where I somehow had access to information that was far more vast than my mind could intellectualise — the same place my visual artwork comes from.

You may have read quotes about being far more amazing than you realise. There is an infinite part of us that is God (or whatever you wish to call it), and when we attune to our divine state, we really can do anything we apply ourselves to. Everything is there, within you, waiting for expression.

Divinatory Meaning

You are invited to explore the state of flow. This card is also a reminder that you are an infinitely amazing being who can access collective consciousness, especially when you surrender some control to the greater process or get out of your own way. You have the permission you felt you needed, so go within and explore. Wonderful gifts are waiting for you.

33. JOURNEY TO WHOLENESS

Self-acceptance, wholeness, unconditional love, soul fragments returning, accepting others as they are, staying energetically present, accepting all parts of self, healing internal dis-ease.

Traditional Japanese painters do not paint the eyes of a deity before the rest of the body, as they say this is the element that brings it to life. But, for this image, I did just that. It was one of the most profound painting experiences I have experienced. I created deep into the night, and no matter how hard I tried, I could not put my paintbrush down. At 3am, I was coaxed away, and as I stepped back, I burst into tears. I was deeply upset at the being that had come alive on the canvas, could be sensed in my art space, and felt as if it was within me.

The canvas held a half-formed being, part woman and somewhat octopus. She was troubled – the process she was in was quite disturbing to her. After doing a clearing, I was able to sleep. The next morning, my housemate inquired what had happened in the night as his pictures were falling off the walls! As I worked on the painting over the next week, it felt like this being was undergoing healing. She was brought to wholeness and became quite beautiful with evolved energy systems and a sense of enlightenment and knowing about her.

I have come to realise that this being is a 'hybrid'. There are mixed reports about what caused these beings to be this way, but it seems there was a distinct sense of upset and disease amongst them, and they had an intense longing to be whole again. Some say the Lemurian hybrids were experiments done by the Atlanteans as they pushed what was possible. Others say they were a result of vibratory similarities as the Lemurians became more physicalised causing them to mix with that of animals, depending on where their vibration was.

Most accounts associate the hybrid form with dis-ease and a sense of being outcast. It is understood that hybrids started appearing toward the end of the Lemurian epoch as they were densifying and the Atlantean mind-based intellect interfered with the ebb and flow of Lemurian ways, though this is not what caused their demise.

Divinatory Meaning

This card is about loving yourself and others from a sense of wholeness, exactly as you are right now. It is only from this space that healing can take place. We may find ourselves in relationships or scenarios where we can see great potential. We may have concepts of others that are not really who they are, due to subconscious projections or ideals. We could have the idea that we will feel better about ourselves when we achieve a goal or status – that success will somehow make everything better. Unfortunately, this takes us out of the present and makes our 'love' somewhat conditional. To be a healer, transcend the perspective that the being in front of you needs to be 'fixed'. Hold the vision that they are perfect as they are. From this place, they can heal themselves through the transformative power of acceptance. Acknowledge the full spectrum of a picture and bring any fractured parts back to the present moment. In this place, we are whole, and thus have the power to step into the brightest version of ourselves.

34. LIFE-FORCE ENERGY

Energy, mana, aina, the rainbow spectrum, bright white light, Reiki, celebrating life, god force, optimal health, being vibrantly alive, thriving nature, conscious consumption, Eden, the body as a temple, bringing Earth into balance, cell rejuvenation, the love of the land.

What happens when we seek to maximise the life-force energy in everything we do? Toward the completion of this oracle deck, I was called to visit Hawaii. I heard it is known to be the last remaining part of the lost continent of Lemuria. I went with an open mind and was sincerely blown away by the incredible level of life-force energy radiated there. I am an avid traveller and seeker of high vibrational places, but had never experienced such potency of the 'magic' (the main inspiration of my art) in every cell of every bright green leaf! I could sense the songs of Lemuria in this pristine place.

I discovered I had been dreaming of this place my whole life. The crystalline waterfalls, rainbow diffused skies, exotic flowers and opulent plant life was so present that you couldn't help but see a radiant aura around everything. 'Aina' is a Hawaiian term for 'energy' and 'sacred land'. It seemed to me that 'mana' and 'aina' are one and the same.

One day, when I was sitting on Red Sand Beach, I had a vision of an overlaying dimension that spanned our physical world. This overlay was the god force or life force in its purest and highest vibration.vThe vision presented an array of objects familiar to this physical plane from lower vibrational concrete, processed chemicals and suffering-imbued consumables, to the higher bio-dynamic earthly offerings and the vibrant lands that surrounded me at that moment.

The experience imprinted the depths of my being with the remembering that we can bring this beautiful blue planet back to its former glory, starting with our own temples and personal pieces of Eden. I realised that maximising one's life-force energy was the gateway to bridging heaven and earth. By aligning our choices with this higher frequency, we will naturally create more opportunities to ground this somehow-forgotten light. When we know the joy of this life force, within and around us, and are vibrantly alive, we can't help but inspire others to choose the same.

Divinatory Meaning

It is time for celebration. Revel in the bliss of being alive! This is an incredibly healing card packed with luminous life-force energy for optimal health and healing. It reminds you to seek joy and upliftment in everything you do – as much as is possible. Consider the foods you eat, the environments you spend your time in, the people in your life, and even the things you wear. Increase your awareness of their journey, how they came to be in your world, and their energetic resonance. Are they alive and vibrant? You may also be inspired to work with healing energies such as Reiki or with the land, perhaps to grow vegetables. You are encouraged to joyously make your life a piece of Eden. As a result, you will shine with vitality.

35. LUMIN ESSENCE

Self-love, the light that radiates from our hearts, light shining in the darkness, heart-centred living, removing your heart armour, accepting your shadows as the flip side of your strengths, a vulnerable wide-open heart, authentic heartfelt needs.

When we choose to journey through life from our hearts, it illuminates the darkness, all illusion drops away, and we see what is real. What does self-love look like for you? Self-love is often talked about, but we don't always consider its deeper implications. One of the keys for bringing heaven to earth is the realisation of our optimal reality. To create a New Earth, not dissimilar to the Lemurian utopia, we navigate or illuminate our journey through our hearts.

When our core foundations are integrity and kindness, our choices are ethical, and our souls radiate warmth, hold compassionate space for others, and inspire others to carry it forward. Unfortunately, as we travel through life, we often armour ourselves to protect our hearts. We fear them to be delicate and vulnerable, but this is contrary to the incredible power of having a fully open heart.

Sadly, we can toss parts of ourselves in the 'trash' because we cannot see how they serve us, or they may feel too ugly or painful. Loving yourself is about accepting all of yourself, including the parts you may consider less desirable. Self-love is unconditional. As we make the journey to wholeness, we see that the parts we have severed from ourselves are counterparts to our greatest strengths.

We also realise the actions we thought benefited others, when we went out of our way to please, fall short or fall away. In their place, we can allow authentic gifts to unfurl and bring luminosity to shared endeavours and environments. Consider how you relate to your world when you come to it from a happy place of fullness, doing things because you want to. Sometimes we feel we must give away our happiness to show we care for others. But, when we live our joy, it affects others. Acting from uninspired obligation and the cloud it brings, can hold no light to that joy!

Remember, your internal world reflects your outer reality. If you are met by less than ideal dynamics, they may hold a clue to your unloved parts. Accepting our less-desirable aspects doesn't make the behaviours that may arise from them okay. Accepting your whole self means being okay with the foundations that created these insecurities and bringing them back into balance.

A technique for painting light involves balancing the surroundings with a darker colour. The darker the juxtaposition, the brighter the light appears. This is a great analogy for accepting all aspects of our deeper selves. Be real with your shadows, so you can let more light in and shine brighter.

Love is the most potent and healing tool that we have, and the more we feel, the more we create. It's contagious too! The more we live from our hearts, the more we find it in our lives. So how do we kickstart this wholeness of being? Be present and authentic with your heartfelt needs. Have an awareness and a softening toward your unloved parts. It may seem easier said than done, but start seeing things from a gentler, more compassionate place, away from judgement. In the bigger picture, we are all doing the best we can within our circumstances.

Often the things that keep us out of our hearts are much

simpler to release than we realise. Finding what makes us happy and surrounding ourselves with those who really 'see' us and encourage us goes a long way. Be aware of the parts of yourself that you find easy to love, and set goals for healing themes that require extra care and attention. Honour the fantastic vessel your body is. Look at what you are good at and grow your self-appreciation from this place. Wonder at the challenges you have moved through. Dream big, but also be real about what is achievable. Do not compare yourself to others, as we all have our different struggles and strengths. Think about all you are grateful for. Acts of kindness are another way to expand that heartfelt feel-good vibe.

Divinatory Meaning

Consider the parts of yourself you may not be accepting. You may be experiencing an inner dissonance due to what you are trying to push away. This card is about self-love. That is, the deep, compassionate, unconditional love of self that brings you into wholeness. Lumin Essence means the essence of light. There is nothing that makes us shine more than a heart that is full of love. You can shine through the shadows most gracefully when there is no fear within. Accept your shadows so they can more easily resolve. Allow more light and love, inside and out of your world.

36. MANIFESTIA

Manifestation, sowing the seeds of your dreams, creating your reality, trusting what you desire is already happening, magic-making, pollinating your wishes, as above, so below.

You can decide how you want to live. The universe is in full support of you choosing to step into the optimal version of yourself. Dream big, then dream bigger. Now is a great time to start the projects you have been considering.

All it takes is some pollination. In the realms of making magic happen, we say, "As above, so below." So, start planting your dream seeds, and nourish the soil with enthusiasm for what can and will be. Feel your dream in its entirety as if it is already happening and then let it go.

Let all sense of control or direction go – do not try to manage it. Feel how beautiful your dream's fruition will be, but then leave it alone to flourish as it will. Any sense of desperation or neediness will only falter its progress. Although the lessons gained as a result of this will bring growth, depending on what you are ready for.

Germinate your dream seeds in the present tense with positive terminology. Rather than thinking in terms of what you don't want, focus on what you do want as if you already have it, as the subconscious will hear the keywords and bring you more of this.

Be creative with your dream visioning. Create symbols from the letters that make up your wish sentence. Incorporate the natural elements that resonate with your manifestation such as fire or earth. Find meaningful symbols that align with your desired outcome, add a rush of energy and charge it with an intention for the greatest good. In meditation, send them off into the heart space of the Aether. Meanwhile, turn the physical soil in real-time. Do the necessary preparation and relax into the knowledge that with your intention, this is enough.

Divinatory Meaning

This card encourages you to dream big. It comes as a reminder that you can choose how you want your life to go. You can manifest all you wish to create or release. It's time to sow the seeds of the reality you want to experience. In magical practice there is a saying, "As above, so below." Work with this principle through affirmative thinking and higher intention. Then, anchor or ground your dream seeds. Manifest from the heart, overcome fear, take strong positive action, and let go of the outcome. Know and trust your dreams are already on their way and expect to see results.

37. MOUNT SHASTA

Your origins, the seeds that make you what and who you, star beings, sacred power places, unexplained mystical phenomena, intuitive messages and downloads, dreams and visions.

Aware that their entire continent would be destroyed, the Lemurians travelled to other parts of the globe. Mount Shasta has a profound connection with the Lemurian people, as it was one place they journeyed. There are many tales of multidimensional beings living inside the mountain, and sightings of all kinds of unusual phenomena here.

When I received the intuitive message that I would be writing and delving more deeply into the emerging theme of these cards, I had a strong vision to visit this mountain and channel a painting on it. After a range of synchronicities, I found myself there. The ambience of this magical place cannot be denied, and the image you see on this card is what came through.

Mount Shasta also seems to have a connection to star beings and portals to multiple worlds and parallel realities. On arrival at Mount Shasta town, I was involved in a Pleiadian channelling circle where I had a vision of the stars communicating with the mountain through light code, and interconnected glowing grid lines lay over the entire Earth. I have experienced these luminescent grid lines before.

I have been told I can put my hand into them and connect my healing light with all the other lights doing their work across the planet. During my time at Mt Shasta, I came to understand there have been many UFO sightings there and I realised how connected the Lemurians were to star beings. Further research revealed several accounts of Lemurians being of mixed origins, from throughout the universe.

This place holds many stories, and I had my insights, but it felt right to keep the imagery for this card simple. I felt as if what was depicted spoke beyond the mind. I was quite perplexed at what the meaning of this card would be. I knew Mount Shasta would be an important card in the deck, but I didn't realise how significant it would be until the following was revealed.

I planned to include symbols on the ten chakra cards that would activate the chakras, but I wasn't sure how. The creation of these cards has been a profound unfolding, and when I sought guidance, I received the message that the chakra activation codes were in this Mount Shasta painting. There was a symbol for each of the chakras, and you can find them on the bottom left-hand side of the chakra cards. This image is the seed crystal that this whole deck is based around.

Divinatory Meaning

This card is about origins. It is time to honour and look more deeply into your ancestry, both your bloodline and your etheric lineage. Do you have an affinity with any star beings? Connecting with them might allow you greater insight into your traits, your strengths and challenges. Perhaps you have a Lemurian connection? This card may also be encouraging you to visit sacred places you feel attracted to. They may have an intuitive message for you.

38. NEW BLUEPRINTS

Be the change, take action, take a step no matter how small, ignite an upward spiral, make a positive change, ethics and compassion, creating a ripple of light.

"Be the change you wish you to see," is an empowering mantra to remind us that we can step up and create the blueprints for the world we want to know. Powerful, meaningful change starts with you today.

Despite our desire to see change, we can be overwhelmed by all that is going on in the world and making a positive impact can seem impossible. It is healthy to have an interest in what is happening around us, but it is important not to become so disheartened that we can't find the inner light to ignite even the tiniest upward spiral of improvement. There is still so much natural beauty on this incredible blue planet, and there are organisations and solo game-changers creating amazing transformation all the time. Shift your focus onto what is possible, rather than what isn't.

Stepping forward with action, however small, will benefit the vibration of the planet, in some way. We have more of a voice than we realise. As consumers, we can direct our energy and make a difference through ethical choices. By stepping out of our own needs and wants, we can help someone less privileged. We can pick up trash, be present with someone or smile at those we share a path with. Small acts create a ripple of goodness in the world.

Consider how all beings can coinhabit this glorious planet. Could you design a blueprint for ethical, compassionate, heart-centred living? What would the guardians of this Earth need to do, need to be? How would they feel about themselves? What can you do to uphold this?

Divinatory Meaning

This card inspires action, no matter how small, that will create a ripple of light in the world. You are part of a bigger picture, a greater story, and your actions, your choices, your presence, are making a difference. You have more power than you realise. Focus on what you can do – and do it well. Change takes time, so make plans and start now.

39. OUR ANCIENT FUTURE

Wisdom from indigenous peoples, ancestors holding the keys for the future, ancient remembering, bloodlines, how the past affects the future, a time to step up, timeless power symbols, activations for powerful shifts.

Right now, the legends of the Lemurian civilisation feel important, as the wisdom from this ancient time is relevant. The fall of Lemuria alerts us to the possibility that humanity may face if we live without respect for the earth. An ancient remembering is emerging. Many of the seed crystals and the knowledge they are imbued with are becoming unearthed. All those who can see a better future are not just dreaming. Their hearts and minds are harkening to the core of earth-based traditions to bring through knowledge that will help shift this paradigm into balance.

It is said that the Lemurians who survived the fall, travelled the planet and ended up in the places where inspiring indigenous knowledge far outweighs what Western minds have come to prioritise. The Ancient Egyptians, Mayans, Inca, Tibetans, Maoris, Indigenous Australians and Hopi are examples. These ancient knowledge keepers of Earth and Aethers have been holding the key for a new world.

We are being called back to our roots to acknowledge the infinite wisdom available when we drop to our knees in humble receptivity. To move gracefully forward, we must first stand in our power for the places, ethics and conservation of what matters most.

When we heal ourselves, we often heal our ancestors, also.

As illuminated beings ready to make a change in the collective consciousness, we can sometimes take on what seems like more than our fair share of karma. We may be clearing some of the wounds from our ancestors. With this in mind, we can ease through the waves, allowing guidance and empowered perspective to lead us to the greatest good.

Divinatory Meaning

This card is imbued with activations for a new paradigm. You are now being showered with blessings in preparation for a transformation. It may be turbulent at times, but you will grow and heal through the coming journey. Partake in activities that help you drop into a meditative state as often as possible. Use clearing tools to raise your vibration and don't get caught up on the destination. Focus on the journey and experience. You can navigate a situation you have no experience with by being truly present. Integrity and intuition will be your guide.

40. RADICAL EXPANSION

Living and loving at full capacity, being unapologetically you, self-expression, boldness, having a voice, taking up space, expansion, empowerment, owning your true power, being visible in the world, having fun with your magnificence, letting go of judgement, creative exploration, radical ways of being.

What would it be like to live, love and feel at full capacity? Do you imagine what it would be like? This card is about being truly and unapologetically you. The gifts you think are too bold for this world and those heartfelt experiences you believe you should hold back on, might just light someone up! The physical self-expression that you dull down so you fit in and those dreams that seem too vast could be precisely what the world is waiting for.

Do you feel you have the right to take up space? Our auras can expand manifold, but we often choose to keep them tight to our bodies – maybe for safety? But what is this construct in which we have imprisoned ourselves? Where does this subtle (or not-so-subtle) shame come from? Why not dance our most beautiful dance, dress in a way that makes us feel magnificent and sing, so our voices are heard?

Considering the paradigm of our judgement in others can help us expand into authentic expression. We may not be aware of the thoughts that were imprinted in us from a young age, through our parents, teachers, society and the media. Separation and limitation begin with your beliefs around what is acceptable and what is not. Connection and possibility come through owning your power and embracing your responsibility to be more visible in the world – to not shy away from life!

It is time for radical ways of being and thinking, and you can start by granting yourself the freedom and creativity to be you. Having a voice is essential for power to shift back to individuals and communities outside of prescribed normality. It is time to unleash your inner rainbow dragon and unapologetically claim your heart-based empowerment and radiantly unconventional gifts – and to have fun with it!

Divinatory Meaning

It is time for expansion. You can be as big as your energy wants to be. Stop and consider anything that is holding you back. This card is the permission slip that allows you to let go of limiting stories and take up all the space you need. Have fun unleashing who you are. As bold and radical as some of your ideas or offerings might be, who is to say they are not what the world is waiting for, what the world *wants!* Take note of any judgement of authentic expression, towards yourself or others. Be mindful that creatively exploring unrefined expression may be what is needed right now. Remember to centre yourself in your heart and be the masterpiece your soul always wanted you to be.

41. REALM BRIDGER

Visionaries, architects of the future, information from other realms, bridging the seen with the unseen, inspiration, seeding a new Earth, traversing different states of consciousness, birthing ideas from subtle reality, journeying.

Have you ever felt that there is more than meets the eye in the perception we call reality? That there is more going on behind the scenes? Do you ever glimpse beyond your physical senses and wonder if what they perceive is just the tip of the iceberg? Do you ever get visions or insights just as you are falling off to sleep? Do you dream in colours that are more vibrant than you have experienced in waking life?

As you raise your vibration and explore different states of consciousness, you may experience phenomena you might have believed only happens in fantasy stories. Through meditation and journeying, we invite a greater awareness of the subtle realities. These realms can be amazing places to bring through pioneering ideas, creativity and to explore the edges of the universe.

This card is about bridging the seen and the unseen. Intuitive painting is my method of connection, but the ability to crystallise the normally intangible can manifest in other ways. Anchoring the collective dreaming for a new future is not as out of reach as we may think. Just as water changes from solid to gas to liquid, we can catch the intangible in other forms. Metaphors, codes or even maths can form the path of the visionary.

Once these visions are in the minds and hearts of many, it can merge into matter. These blueprints then go to the architects, and the ideas become physicalised. It is time to dream outside the box. It is time for the inventors, the artists, the poets, and the visionary leaders to step forward and collectively dream in a new future.

Divinatory Meaning

You are the pioneer of your life. The way forward may be in your dreams or visions. You might find it useful to do automatic writing or intuitive drawing to capture some of the more lucid information. Be creative, and don't take on the opinions of others. It's time to think and do things a whole other way. After all, as the saying goes, "Insanity is doing the same thing over and over and expecting a different result."

42. RECLAIM YOUR ENERGY

Recapitulation, owning your power, where you put your energy is your choice, overcoming triggers through self-awareness, energy vampires, reclaiming your soul fragments, observing the observer, shifting victim mentality.

When we embrace an energy-aware lifestyle, we start to notice when we feel drained or ungrounded. We may feel flat or out of our centre after spending time with certain people or places. Our energy is our responsibility, and how we give it away becomes a conscious choice as we step into empowerment. But, what about the fragments of self we gave away before we came to this awareness? Yes, it is possible to recover and restore yourself to wholeness. In shamanic practice, recapturing and reuniting with lost fragments of our selves is called 'recapitulation.'

Even when we become aware of the patterning that unnecessarily chews up our energy, we may still feel drained by certain people or situations. When we grow our awareness further and take note of the triggers, we see it is always our choice where our energy goes, although it might not feel that way.

We may feel we need to give to the people we most care about, in a way that depletes us. We may hold a subconscious sense of obligation to others, or a belief that our own needs cannot be met until we have taken care of everyone else. We may run ourselves ragged meeting deadlines, keeping customers happy, living up to expectations, or ensuring we have everything our children require from us. Many of us expend energy through drama, self-doubt, self-sabotage, anxiety and fear. Sometimes we sense we are giving too much (but cannot see exactly how it is happening) or that our effort may be unproductive, even counterproductive. But it doesn't have to be like this.

To claim more time and energy for yourself, look at what is and isn't serving you. You may need to make changes in your external environment. More often, the most effective change will be to your perception of self. What beliefs and learnings serve you? What fear-based and limiting expectations are keeping you from your power? Consciously choose and align yourself with ideas that serve you, and suddenly you will have a lot more energy for the meaningful, inspiring parts of your life. You will also have improved presence and more for your loved ones.

We become aware of our patterning through self-awareness. By observing the observer, we can broaden our perspective of how and why we react to certain stimuli. This understanding helps us untangle ourselves from drama. We can distinguish what is relevant and real to us in the here and now from outdated stories. Instead of reacting when we feel triggered, we can peel back the layers of those moments and claim greater understanding of ourselves and the myths we have unwittingly subscribed to, or that others have ascribed to us. Meditation can help us explore and take responsibility for our internal dissonance. Anything that takes you out of the busy-ness of your mind can heighten your perspective so you can see the bigger picture.

There are other contributors to energy depletion, such as not having enough healthy food or sleep. Diet and lifestyle are usually easier to rebalance than our self-beliefs. Illness and environments that affect self-esteem or where our soul does not feel at home or safe are other factors. We may need outside help to reclaim our energy, but having an awareness of what is required is a step closer to being able to fix the problem, and can start the healing process. When you are going through tough times, doing something that makes the soul rejoice, even something small, is extremely helpful in boosting your energy levels.

Divinatory Meaning

This card encourages you to be aware of where your energy is going. If you are not at your optimal energy level, it invites you to consider the core of why this may be. You have the power to own your energy and choose where you direct it. Look at situations that trigger drama and anxiety to reduce energy loss. Detach from environments or people that are not healthy for you. It is up to you to make the shift. Victim mentality is no help, so realise you have the power to transform your life and choose healing and self-empowerment. It's time to kickstart the upward spiral to abundant energy and soul presence.

43. SHE OF THE LOTUS

Shadow work, addressing dissonance, seeing downfalls as the flipside of superpowers, loving yourself back to wholeness, the beautiful lotus that grows from murky waters, disempowering triggers, bringing light into your dark corners.

Originally, the title for this oracle deck was going to be *The Language of Light.* It was not actualised in that incarnation as other layers of meaning needed to be honoured — the fuller spectrum I was guided to bring through also included the shadow. In hindsight, choosing to deepen the message of balance that the Lemurians were bringing forth through this work meant I had to experience my shadow.

My shadow encounters brought light into nooks I didn't know I had. If there is a way to fast track your growth, it is by being real with the shadowy or unloved parts of ourselves. There was a time when the concepts of 'shadow work' and 'self-love' seemed relevant, but I was vague as to what they really meant. I knew the next part of my journey was exploring them, but how that would happen was quite mystifying. The shadow and self-love are big topics to unpack and unravelling them took me on quite an adventure. Unfortunately, I thought shadow work was about digging up as many issues as possible and that being 'present with them' meant wallowing in them. Without tools for expanded awareness, I found myself drowning deeper in the upset of it all and creating more of it in the process.

My journey for clarity took me to Cambodia, where I met and mastered the art of perspective and indirectly finding growth points in a way that spoke to my being rather than my mind. That sparked a three-month journey into the farthest reaches of myself. I realised I had a lot of unlearning and self-acceptance to do. The years of trying to be the best that I could be created constructs in my self-identity. My striving wasn't as healthy as I'd thought. By discarding traits that seemed ugly or hindering, I was also rejecting sides of myself that were quite wonderful. They were two sides of the coin, and equally, they were part of my true nature.

When we discard any part of ourselves, we are throwing the baby out with the bathwater. Often our greatest strengths are our greatest weaknesses and vice versa. When we reject or deny parts of ourselves, we end up feeling hollow, lost and detached. When we take them out of the trash and work with them through compassion, gentleness, honesty and non-judgement, we can shine a light on these shadows and see them for what they are. Incredibly, my perceived weaknesses vanished as I peeled the layers further and further back, to explore the past experiences that accompanied them. Accepting the shadows enough to bring them into the daylight was usually all it took for them to dissipate. Their power dissolved and I could see them for what they were, or rather were not.

Paradoxically, self-love is a catalyst for transformation. Alchemising painful triggers is an opportunity for awareness that helps us reclaim more of ourselves. As the dense spaces begin to evaporate, we can be filled with more light, more love, and we create an upward healing spiral.

I have come to learn that shadow work and self-love are practices to implement on a day-to-day basis. When we merge this awareness with moment-to-moment consciousness, densities don't even get a chance to form. We can then live and love even bigger! And, this is true freedom, self-empowerment and where authentic love and light can radiate.

A true light bringer shines light in all the corners so shadows can be acknowledged and released.

Divinatory Meaning

Take a look at any unconscious patterns that may be running you. Are there elements of yourself you need to take out of the trash, dust off and reabsorb? Shadows can be painful or tender to the touch. 'Sensitivity' in an area can be a 'trigger' that shows us where we might want to spring clean some of our darker forgotten, ignored or hidden corners. Accepting our shadows is the first stage in restoring ourselves to wholeness, in self-love. Peel back the layers where there is shame, guilt or fear and bring them into the daylight. Under a loving and compassionate light, they will resolve and reassimilate so you can re-engage with your superpowers.

44. SHINE YOUR LIGHT

Doing what you love, time to thrive, giving from the overflow, life purpose, being authentically you, compassionate self-empowerment, loving life, trying things you resonate with, bringing joy to others by being an inspiration.

You are amazing, there is no one like you, and no one can do 'you' as you can. Yet, we sometimes feel that we need to be a certain way — a way not aligned with our authentic self.

You may feel obliged to be something or someone. You may have stopped doing some of the things you love due to time or energy restraints. When you take time to do what truly makes you shine each day, you will light up and bring joy to other people's worlds. As you go about your life, you will have a sense of purpose and feel naturally inspired to fulfil your responsibilities. You will also have more energy and love to overflow.

Doing what we love can bring so much goodness to our hearts that it filters into other areas of our life. Yet when life is demanding more of us, we give up the things we love, to make way for more 'practical' pursuits. When we finally come back to these pursuits, we wonder why we waited.

For much of my life, I did not paint, as I thought it was self-indulgent. I questioned how doing what I love could be beneficial to others. Now, the constant messages of gratitude I receive for anchoring my visions on canvas make me wonder how I ever thought that way!

It takes discipline to do what we love, especially if we are natural givers. It is easy to get caught up with other people's lives. There can also be a strong cultural belief that fulfilling a creative need is selfish. The irony here is that tending to our own needs, harms none, and we will have a lot more to give.

It is time for us to collect our light and shift the vibration here on Earth – starting with our inner sense of being. Try those things you have always wanted to explore. Weave enjoyment through your day-to-day experience. Find purpose and the inspiration to spring out of bed in the morning. It is time to thrive.

Divinatory Meaning

Where can you shine your light? When you have a purpose, you will also have limitless energy and know joy. Where can you grow enthusiasm in your life? Consider how you can be more aligned with your passions so you can harness your light. It may be time to return to something you enjoyed but stopped doing, for no good reason. You are a sovereign being, regain compassionate empowerment and remember what lights up your world.

45. STAR SEED ELEMENTAL

Children as teachers, fun, light-heartedness, joy, laughter, newly incarnated souls, the child within, maintaining an inquisitive perspective, wonder and imagination.

Being with children can be a great way to recapture wonder, innocence, unapologetic truth and wisdom. Their realities are not yet muddied by shoulds or cannots, and their imaginations are often so wild and creative that they can be our biggest inspirers. Furthermore, as their incarnation from pure spirit is more recent, they are still aware of energy and have a natural psychic awareness.

Sometimes 'adulting' can become too serious. When this happens, bringing a childlike, light-hearted sense of play to your perspective can be the most productive way to rebalance. Facing challenging circumstances with inquisitiveness can bring joy to whatever we are accomplishing. Imagine stepping into a child's shoes and seeing how they perceive the world. If you have a problem, consider how a child might solve it.

Think back to when you were little and what you loved to do. Remember how the world felt around you and how magical and mysterious things may have been. What has changed? What would you tell the seven-year-old you? The little people of today will be the inventors, creators, and leaders of tomorrow. How can we help nourish their big souls, to ready them for an optimal journey through life?

Right now, powerful souls are incarnating on Earth to help with the progression of this planet. All children are equally special, but some may have different or unique needs due to their more sensitive and energetic natures. The ways children were brought up in previous generations may not be the best options for today. Humans are evolving, and children can be our wisest teachers. May we listen to them with our hearts and let their ways unveil fresh new eyes so we may see a whole new world.

Divinatory Meaning

Bring a sense of play, lightness or spontaneity to your life. Be inspired by children or your inner child. You are encouraged to add inquisitiveness, fun and laughter to your reality. This card may signify the presence of a child in your life. Spending time with children will help you experience the world from a fresh perspective and see them as the inspiring teachers they are.

46. STAR SEER

Listen to your intuition, trust the holistic journey, dreams finding their way into being, the bigger picture, a more aligned outcome than expected, clarity of the greater path.

Have you ever headed toward a specific destination, but instead of it being where you ended up, the journey was the catalyst for getting you where you were meant to go? Have you ever felt the universe was conspiring against you, and nothing seemed to be working out as planned, but then everything came together in a way that was so perfect? This card is about the journey not going as planned, but the outcome being better than you thought possible.

When we set our dreams and intentions, internal or external shifts may need to occur before we start to see results. Outdated doors may need to close. Ideas that are holding you back may need to transform.

Life's winding roads may make it seem as though you are off the path, despite how right your decisions may feel. Trust and know that your higher self may have bigger plans for you. There might be some adventures on the way – or not. The road you take depends on how ready you are and the distance between your current life and one you are dreaming into being.

This card depicts intuition as a goddess. She is lifting you out of the clouds of confusion and mind noise and showing you the clear way forward. She is your higher self and can see your great potential. Trust your instincts and have faith in your dream. You are already on your way.

Divinatory Meaning

Keep believing in yourself. Trust in your dreams enough to let the serendipities unfold. Let go enough to allow space for unexpected opportunities. Even when the route is not as direct as you imagined, listen to your intuition, and know you have got this!

47. STEPPING THROUGH

Follow your heart, dream big, stepping through something that has been holding you back, the threshold, starting new projects, self-belief, it is all possible, the road less travelled, trust.

Step in and step up all those dreams or projects you have been putting off. Now is the time to start, even if it is just one small element of the bigger picture. Although "just do it" has been coined by a commercial brand, it is one of my fundamental mantras. We will always have myriad reasons why today isn't the day but remember: Opportunity dances with those already on the dance floor (H. Jackson Brown, Jr.).

When you start something, talk about it, take consistent steps to actualise it, and you will see it take on a momentum of its own. The right people, places and opportunities will magnetise, and it will start to come together. Don't be afraid to fail. The success we see around us has come from perseverance. Falling and getting back up again is part of the journey. Focus your energies and commit to seeing your vision become a reality. You are human, so set reasonable expectations, and know that when you apply yourself, you can make amazing things happen. Building a dream can seem overwhelming, but if you break it down and make a plan, you will gracefully find a way through.

You might be able to manage most aspects of a project, and it is great to have an incentive to learn more skills, but it doesn't mean you need to do it on your own. Whatever you are aiming to achieve, there are people out there with the tools, skills and energy you may be missing. Look at the bigger picture and delegate. A mentor, people on a similar journey or an accountability buddy can be wonderful supporters and allies.

Following your dreams is fulfilling and empowering, but as it is often a path less travelled, you may need to plot your own course or invent a way through. Also, consider what kind of lifestyle you would like and know this may change and evolve as you do.

What you can do, or dream you can, begin it,
Boldness has genius, power, and magic in it.
— John Anster, inspired by Johann Wolfgang von Goethe

Divinatory Meaning

The time is now. No more excuses or tomorrows. Whatever you have been putting off, the universe is now pushing you to make it happen. You may feel a little outside your comfort zone, but that is where the magic happens. Take a leap! Combine your intuition with a plan of action. Break it down and trust the puzzle will come together, piece by piece, through the courageous act of making a start.

48. SURRENDER

Trust, letting go of control, free flow, receptivity, yin energy, inner knowing, intuition, synchronistic opportunities, getting out of your way, the path of least resistance, allowing who you naturally are to flourish.

Surrendering can be one of the hardest things to do. Trusting that we can achieve more by loosening our control can take great courage. Sometimes the most constructive way forward is to stop forcing things into being. Rather than allowing, inviting and drawing a project into being, the energy here is of frustration as if you are pushing something heavy up a mountain. At these times, gravity or 'flow' don't seem to be on your side. Use this awareness as a guide when you start to detour from your path.

When control is released, so too is resistance. One of the biggest skills we can learn is to get out of our own way. When we are in a receptive place, we are open to a world of opportunities and the great mysteries can unveil themselves. The mind loves to control the outcome, but this only creates limitations. It can feel scary, but when we allow ourselves to be 'caught' by the universe, myriad possibilities open to us.

This painting is called A Star is Born, and its message is about becoming the star you came here to be. You can reach your peak life experience through surrendering and allowing who and what you truly are to flourish. Today, be more, by doing and trying less. This advice goes against the grain of our striving culture that encourages us to source from outside ourselves and to busy ourselves out of a natural state of all-knowing bliss.

Surrender is a key element in the creative process. When I let go and flow, allowing intuition over direction, I find I create far more powerful works.

That is not to say our lives should be left to the slipstream. The message is about freeing ourselves from the paradigm of control and force. Yes, we can achieve with this mode, but we also lose opportunities for magic. A synchronistic meeting, following our intuition and being in the right place at the right time, can outweigh months of careful planning.

Divinatory Meaning

Loosen your hold on the reins and know the universe will catch you. Trust, even though things are not as you imagined. Stay poised and aligned with your purpose. At the last minute, the situation will reveal its magic.

49. THE INFINITE

The eternal life force, cycles of growth, rising from the ashes, mini deaths and rebirths within one's life, you are so much more than your physical body.

The beings in Lemuria are said to have lived for many hundreds of years. As they were only partially incarnated, their bodies were much lighter, less physically actualised and less affected by ageing. They were also aware of their infinite nature. The Lemurians were multidimensional beings and regularly traversed realms other than the physical, including the places before and after 'death.'

As we become aware that we are so much more than our physical bodies, we may experience a sense of the eternal. Thus, fear around death gives way to recognising new beginnings, so we remember what is real, and focus on what we wish for this life. Whatever we believe will happen when our body goes back to the earth, we can live to the fullest while we are here, in this incarnation.

You may feel like you have led many lives and expressed different faces to the world. We can experience many mini-deaths and re-births as we allow outdated parts of ourselves to fall away. When we choose to align our lives with our spirit, we may find we experience more of these mini deaths. They can be daunting but are fast-tracking our growth to prepare us for the shining new chapter that beckons.

Divinatory Meaning

This card of rebirth can appear after challenges that have required a level of surrender. You have arrived at a beginning. Revel in your newfound inner freedom. Blockages have fallen away, doors are opening, and there are opportunities to step into. Stretch your wings and see how far they can reach. Rise from the ashes, like a phoenix, born anew ready for a new cycle of growth. Celebrate, honour the road that brought you here, and prepare to take flight with the tools you have gathered through your elevation process.

50. THE PORTAL KEEPER

Unique gateways to mystical experiences, psychic ability, raising your vibration, expanded consciousness, the Akashic records, past-life ties, exploring the edges of reality for significant messages, seeing between the lines, multidimensional awareness.

As we become more sensitive and aware, we are more receptive to mystical experience. We can realise there are overlaying realities that seem just as real, if not more vibrant and profound, than the familiar everyday one. There is a theory that space and time are constructs that allow our human minds to grasp sequences in chronological order and enable us to orientate and move forward through reality. In their current evolution, humans are only using a small portion of their brain capacity. If we unlock our mind's potential, what would we fathom that we can't now? There is information out there that isn't real to us until we glimpse it with our senses.

The beings of Lemuria evolved with a different kind of intelligence. They were skilled at harnessing energy from natural and abundant forces such as crystals, the heart of the earth, and the moon. They could share complex information without words. The Lemurians operated in multiple realms at will and could disappear from human perception. Technically, they were in the same location but in an overlaying reality, a parallel dimension which could be very different.

Psychically advanced people can sense discarnate souls, elementals in nature and spirit guides. They can also see information in energy fields. These perceptions (clairvoyance, clairsentience or clairaudience) are still connected to this reality but are examples of what can happen when we raise our consciousness or train ourselves to the subtleties of what is happening around us. In essence, we share our physical location with overlaying beings and energies and can raise or lower our vibration to match and enter their realms of reality.

Two people in an identical environment can have different experiences. One may thrive and enjoy the opportunities of the moment. The other may see only the negatives in the situation. Here, one or both parties may be traversing realities on a micro-level. These micro realms may look very similar, but the way we feel, the reflections we see in others and the way circumstances unfold are aligned with our vibration. So, it's great to be conscious of our energy and the ways we can optimise our experience of life. Like attracts like. It is important to keep this in mind if you are considering traversing deeper realms as it is an endless rabbit hole. Set your energy field to the highest good and ensure your intention is primed for the places you wish to journey to.

Traversing other realms is an innate ability that we all have. Young children have this skill intact as they are not yet convinced that it is not real. Animals, especially cats, also have this awareness. People who experience hallucinations may be perceiving multiple layers of information simultaneously. In the West, this may be considered a symptom of diminished mental health. In other cultures, this openness could be the mark of a shaman or seer and considered a powerful gift.

The Akashic paradigm combines multidimensionality with the idea that everything is happening simultaneously. Thus, everything that has ever been and ever will be is occurring at this moment. By changing our vibration, we can access an ocean of collective consciousness, and this highlights the significance of portals.

Portals are gateways to other layers of reality. They can be accessed through meditation and inner practices, or externally in places such as the planet's vortices. These places are usually sacred to those who are sensitive to energies and work closely with the earth. Often where ley lines connect, portals are places where the veil is thin and unexplainable phenomena can occur.

Earth's ley lines are similar to the meridian systems on the body. Chakras are also energetic vortexes. When we tune to them, and the places on the body they connect to, we can access holistic information. This oracle deck includes ten chakra seed cards which can activate these portals on the body.

Portals are like an opening or rip in our usual veil of reality. If you feel pulled to explore this curious and vast topic further, it is wise to seek a mentor who is confident traversing these realities. However, simply understanding that there are dimensional layers can help you see between the lines, present in the knowledge that this reality is a fraction of the bigger picture.

How are you connected to your mystical self? How might you raise your vibration to access information that isn't normally perceivable? How can you lift your spirits and soar into wider awareness so you can see life from a heightened perspective? When our minds get out of the way, we can reach the bliss state of the seamless unspeakable where the need for a linear life drops away, and we can centre ourselves through a sense of eternal being.

Divinatory Meaning

Gently explore the edges of your reality. Spend time in the forest to listen, deepen your meditation practice, dance yourself into ecstasy, explore psychic tools and study new healing modalities. If you feel lacking in purpose, or life seems a little mundane, remember there is never a reason to be bored. What we experience with our physical senses is just the tip of the iceberg. Magic exists wherever you care to find it. Look between the lines to limitless discovery.

51. THE SOUND OF THE UNIVERSE

Life-changing experiences, glimpsing the great mystery, significant timing, pivotal moments, the Sri Yantra, the 'tuning fork' of universal consciousness, music, transcending mundane reality.

This card signifies those pivotal moments that transcend belief, remind us of a greater reality and influence us so that life will never be the same again. When I started channelling paintings, I explored sacred geometry by including it as a key element in my creations, without knowing much about its meaning. When I looked up the wisdom of the Sri Yantra, I was blown away. It symbolises the sound of the Universe.

This painting was crucial for me, as it was my make-or-break decider for whether I could fulfil my dream as a painter. It was also significant as I crashed my car trying to steady the painting and momentarily taking my eyes off the road. The events that followed delivered the most spiritual growth I had experienced in this lifetime, up until that point. Interestingly, this piece has also vanished.

The Sri Yantra is a powerful symbol, described as the tuning fork that connects us to universal consciousness. It is present in those aha moments – the fragments in time when life as we know it falls away to reveal a place outside mundane. It brings a sense of awe and overwhelms, and yet it feels so real that it jolts us back to our core for deeper remembering. It allows us to fathom our limitlessness.

This card is also about music as a sacred tool. It speaks of the importance of having a soundtrack for our journey. Music was an essential aspect of ceremony in Lemuria as it bridged the gap between matter and non-matter. Even in this dimension, music opens the portals to an array of feelings and atmospheres. Bring more music into your life to expand your experience and shift your sense of ordinary reality.

Divinatory Meaning

Having your world shaken up, even a little, can invite a deeper glimpse of the great mystery of your life. There are myriad ways to peek behind the veil of the mundane world – ecstatic dance, spiritual exploration and intuitive creative pursuits are just a few. Aim to naturally imbue this awareness in your everyday existence so you can avoid the sudden wake-up calls. Wake up to the hidden music, harmony and wonder of your multidimensional world.

52. THE VIOLET FLAME

Your psychic toolkit, re-centring practices, deepening your energetic awareness, clearing your aura, healthy energetic boundaries, protection, removing trauma from your field, maintaining a high vibration, rebalancing after times of raised frequency.

As we deepen our spiritual path, step out of illusory constructs, and become self-realised empowered beings, life may present us with more opportunities to grow than before. When we explore our innate healing ability, we may experience our expanding consciousness as deeply blissful and illuminating. Our glimpses of higher awareness can be followed by periods of intensity as we return to 'normal'. These uncomfortable experiences are shadow elements, unaligned with the higher vibration, dropping away so we can maintain our new frequency.

Your sensitivity will be heightening, so it may be harder to spend time in places with frantic activity. You may feel disorientated, have emotional ups and downs and even physical symptoms. Daily practices for re-centring will allow you to drop into yourself, and be present and still, away from busy mind chatter and distractions. There are so many ways to meditate, so experiment and find something that works for you. There is no way to do it wrong. Yoga, chi gong, painting or walking, are just a few examples.

We can learn to protect and maintain the energy we cultivate in ourselves. Not from fear, but through a healthy awareness of what is ours and what is the energy of others. As we expand our consciousness, our empathy may increase. Maintaining energetic sovereignty will allow for heartfelt exchanges with healthy boundaries.

Just as we keep our body fit and healthy, it is good to ensure our energy field is free from anything that no longer serves us. We all experience some level of trauma as we go through life. The effects can stay in our aura, and if unaddressed, may influence our physical or emotional wellbeing. There are many ways to clear your energy field. Seeing an energetic healer or learning clearing methods you can do yourself, can be so helpful when you feel dense, heavy, triggered, sluggish or down. Being able to kickstart a positive vibration so you can regain perspective can be the key to flowing through situations that seemed overwhelming or unsurmountable. Work with the violet flame to transmute anything that is not for your highest good into love. The flame is simple to visualise and a powerful tool that can be used by anyone.

Divinatory Meaning

Consider your psychic toolkit. Do you have a range of accessible go-to practices for re-centring, cleansing your aura, and protecting your energy? An exercise routine for psychic fitness will keep your aura strong and resilient, your energy sovereign, and your vibration high. Maintaining clear and vibrant energy will also help you see through illusions that may be blocking or disorienting you. Bring the violet flame into your meditation and self-care practices for graceful rebalance after heightened energy levels.

53. TRANSFORMATION

Self-nurturing, going within, time alone, being present with your feelings, cocooning, before the butterfly, being gentle on yourself, angelic embrace.

This painting started with the name, I needed a hug, so I painted one. During the creation process, the image underwent a profound transformation that paralleled the journey I was taking deep within myself.

This card signifies going inwards and being truly present with wherever you are at in your process. It emits a sense of self-nurture and space that is held as a container for our delicate and vulnerable gestation periods.

The final image is filled with blessings, like an angelic embrace. This care emanates from the being, implying that she is creating it for herself. The most powerful healing comes from a place of presence and acceptance for all that doesn't try to fix anything or push things away.

Divinatory Meaning

Feel whatever you need to feel. It may be hard to be present with some parts of yourself. Bring them into a cocoon of gentle self-love and reflection, and insight will come, the shadows can be released, and your heart space will soften. Cry or be angry if this is what you are holding onto, and laugh at the hilarious, ironic, divine perfection of it all. This card beckons you beyond your constructed outer self where you can delve into the beautiful abyss of your being. Revel in the twilight before the dawn and let your wings unfurl.

54. TRUST YOUR INNOCENCE

Truth, trusting yourself, being real with people, knowing the difference between intuition and paranoia, uncensored feelings, returning to innocence.

It can be hard to decipher between intuition and what our mind is telling us. Stories, projections, expectations, or fear can arise under the guise of intuition. To distinguish truthful inner guidance from paranoia, we must return to innocence, to our purest essence. Here we have access to the truth of our being.

What were the very first feelings or visions you had when you considered the question at hand; before you second-guessed yourself? How does it feel in your body when you are brutally honest with yourself? Try to go beyond the layers of what you have been taught to believe about yourself. When some of the logic falls away, what answers remain?

When you ask a young child a question, they don't censor their answers. Their honesty may not be considered polite or socialised. It may even seem a bit funny. But, it's their truth, and it's interesting to note how intuitive children naturally are.

To tell the difference between intuition and mind chatter, you need to recognise a clear instinctive 'yes' and a distinctive 'no'. For this, you must trust yourself. The foundation of self-trust is honesty. You must be completely honest with yourself, about what feels good, true and real to you, and what does not.

Honesty is more than not lying to yourself. It is also about not withholding information. It is about having deep transparency within yourself. Some might describe their intuitive 'yes' as a softening rather than a feeling of tightening, contracting or avoidance. If we are to stay on our optimal path, trusting our original innocence or instincts is key.

Divinatory Meaning

Learn to trust your inner-sense or intuition. You are encouraged to be absolutely honest with yourself. Cast aside any mind stories and shoulds that you tell yourself. In your heart of hearts you know the answers, dare to listen and to honour them. This card may also relate to being truthful with another person. Relationships can only deepen when we can be real with each other. Consider your timing and be considerate, but this is a time for truths.

55. UNIQUE GIFTS

Your superpowers, a sense of purpose, the meaning behind your quirks, exploring your interests, 'shortcomings' as unique undiscovered skills.

I passionately believe that we all have gifts to bring to the world. If we all did what we truly excelled in and enjoyed, our talents and abilities would enable our communities and our planet to thrive. What would the world be like if each person contributed from a place of overflowing enjoyment, without obligation? Where would we be if the jigsaw pieces came together for a diverse and complementary reality, free from prejudice or competition?

Some of us have already discovered – or remembered – what we feel we are here to do. Others are still seeking or just starting to consider this idea. Your inspiration may come as a message in a vision or dream. It may be something others have recognised in you for a long time. It may come from a deep resonance with something you are yet to try. You may be concerned it will affect – or transform – your current lifestyle. Your gift, or purpose, maybe something you enjoyed immensely as a child but did not bring into your adult life. Perhaps there is an array of 'shoulds' holding you from what you love doing.

When there is enjoyment in what you do, you can give more to it, way beyond your usual capacity. It lights you up when you think or talk about it, and you need less in your life as you are fulfilled through doing it. When you don't do it, you might feel ungrounded or low in energy.

If you haven't connected with your purpose, look at your

quirks and what they are telling you. You may struggle with some things because your mind works differently in these areas. Things you may have considered shortcomings might be the qualities that enable your gifts.

I struggled with dyslexia, and my synaesthesia is so strong that there was always a process of translation when I went outside learned or socialised communication. I had to decipher concepts and thoughts from luminescent abstract images, that amplified the more energy there was behind them. It was quite frustrating, as I felt it made me seem unintelligent. The words I could muster felt inferior to the information I was experiencing. The time it took to translate meant much was lost, so I would often give up mid-sentence.

However, this non-linear way of navigating reality was perfect for energy healing and traversing realms. When I discovered painting, these skills were even more helpful. I then realised I could explain everything in a visual way that included the flow and colour of a feeling, and somehow people all over the world seemed to understand.

Divinatory Meaning

What makes you unique? Any quirks that you feel are shortcomings could be the key to your superpowers. Look for the positive sides of your oddities and traits. How would you like to spend more time? Are there things you would like to try or feel a pull to explore? Now is the time to follow these whispers – you never know how transformational they may be.

56. VULNERABILITY

Real strength, holding space, healing past wounds, accepting yourself as you are, sharing from the depths of your heart, raw truths, compassion for others, removing your armour.

Our vulnerability can be one of the greatest gifts we can share. It can also be the hardest. In our society we are conditioned to put on a façade, to be strong, even in times of difficulty. Paradoxically, being vulnerable is one of the strongest things we can be.

It is easy to armour ourselves from the harsh truths that may be too painful to bring to the light of day. However, this causes greater suffering as buried pain becomes shadows. Unprocessed negative experiences can incarnate as much more troublesome traits or insecurities than their origin.

When we are truly honest with ourselves, in all our facets, we are vulnerable. That honesty is an important step in discovering our shadows and bringing them into the light for healing. Furthermore, when we share our vulnerabilities with others, we allow them to glimpse a deeper part of ourselves. This is fertile soil for trust. It plants the seeds for others to share the places that are most raw or tender for them. Our closest friendships can be formed in this space.

The times when we feel too uncomfortable to reach out to others can be the very times we need them most. Having compassion and awareness of the struggle and disorientation others may be going through is a valuable contribution to the world. Holding space where others can be vulnerable is a key element of healing work. Self-love is also connected to our ability to be vulnerable as it allows us to be true to ourselves, exactly as we are without judgement.

Divinatory Meaning

Be vulnerable with yourself or others. It may also be time to step into the role of healer and hold space. Holding space means being fully present, without judgement, in a way that provides a safe and nurturing environment. In this place, guards can be dropped, and a deeper level of awareness and relating can unfold. Enabling unconditional love and acceptance allows for vulnerabilities to be expressed, for the core of dis-ease to be discovered, and for profound healing to take place.

About Izzy Ivy

IZZY IVY is always delving in the creative side of otherworldly realms, and her truest inspiration is sharing the treasures of her journey in her paintings. Her art gives voice to her mystical experiences, adventures and all she encounters in her spiritual and healing work.

Many of Izzy's creations are conceived through dance. Unique beings start to weave their light through the free flow of movement. The process unravels further once she is back in front of the canvas, and information unfurls in richly coloured, inviting worlds with welcoming guardians.

Izzy is passionate about reminding her audience that magic does exist and that we all hold the codes for becoming the greatest version of our selves. She believes in making art accessible through wearable creations, exhibiting in unusual spaces, live painting and capturing and anchoring energy on canvas.

Fusing childlike innocence with all-knowing depth and strength in her characters, Izzy combines art with the spirit that dances her. Every image is seeded with subtle symbolism for the collective dreaming and keys to a deeper remembering.

Recently, Izzy found her voice in the form of the written word. Her devotion to sharing the Lemurian wisdom and intuitive information that wants to reveal itself right now has given her the passion to explore this form of expression and thus, this guidebook has unfurled as a companion to her paintings.

www.izzyivyart.com
Instagram: **@izzy_ivy_art**

Also available from Blue Angel Publishing

Oracle of the Hidden Worlds

LUCY CAVENDISH
Artwork by Gilbert Williams

Connect with the Wisdom and Healing of the Divine Realms of Heaven and Earth

Beyond this world, just out of sight, lie wondrous realms you may have glimpsed, imagined, remembered or visited in dreams. These other worlds exist behind the veils, to protect and preserve their knowledge and energies. They are slowly revealing themselves, allowing themselves to be experienced and discovered, remembered and restored. Enter the visionary artwork of Gilbert Williams and embark on a marvellous journey into secret spaces and magickal places with bestselling author Lucy Cavendish as your personal guide.

Discover light temples, liminal pathways, Lemurian relics, Camelot's mysteries and more! These worlds may be hidden, but their magick, glory and wisdom are within your reach.

ISBN: 978-1-925538-66-3
44-card and 132-page guidebook set, packaged in a hardcover box.

White Light Oracle

ALANA FAIRCHILD
Artwork by A. Andrew Gonzalez

Enter the Luminous Heart of the Sacred

You have a light within you. Trust in that light and in your own courage. The light is strong enough to guide, support and empower you to fulfil your sacred purpose of healing and soulful manifestation.

White light holds all the frequencies needed for healing ourselves, each other, our planet and all her precious creatures. It is divine medicine for the soul, empowering the heart, clarifying the mind, and awakening higher consciousness. This light is within you and all around you. You were born to be that light. The Universe rallies to encourage, inspire and embolden you to manifest your sacred destiny.

This 44-card and guidebook set features luminous imagery from visionary artist A.Andrew Gonzalez and enlightening messages with signature healing processes from bestselling author Alana Fairchild to help you integrate the loving soul medicine of white light.

Take your journey with complete trust, enjoying the divine beauty of your path, and knowing the light is always with you, revealing the way.

ISBN: 978-1-925538-75-5
44-card and 240-page guidebook set, packaged in a hardcover box.

Also available from Blue Angel Publishing

Whispers of the Ocean Oracle Cards

ANGELA HARTFIELD
Artwork by Ekaterina Golovanova

Immerse Yourself in the Wisdom of the Deep

Enjoy the flow and master the currents of your life with playful dolphins, patient seahorses, regenerative starfish and other fascinating marine beings. Ask a question, shuffle the cards and tap into the intelligence and grace of our planet's rich, healing and revitalising oceans for divination, direction and decision-making.

This sumptuous new collaboration from Angela Hartfield and Ekaterina Golovanova delves beneath the surface and connects you with ancient, knowing and wondrous companions so you can draw on greater strength, replenish your reserves, turn the tide on uncertainty and emerge with clarity, purpose and confidence. Powerful, versatile and sensitive, *Whispers of the Ocean* will help you ride the waves of life so you can come out on top.

Dive into this gloriously illustrated 50-card deck and guidebook set and marvel at the beauty, forgotten treasures and hidden wonders within you.

ISBN: 978-1-925538-73-1
50-card and 124-page guidebook set, packaged in a hardcover box.